VIC

EVERY FALL

THE ANTAEUS APPROACH TO OVERCOME DISABILITIES

KURT WARNER

WILKES-BARRE

ISBN-13 978-1-964205-01-4

Library of Congress Control Number: 2024947422

Kallisti Publishing Inc. titles may be bulk purchased for business or promotional use or for special sales. Please see *https://www.KallistiPublishing.com/special-sales/* for more information.

For any lexicographers or philologists into whose hands this book may fall, the publisher may or may not have incorporated into the text, as a stimulus and a challenge to your perspicacity, one or more deliberate errors. If you'd like to alert us to your discovery, please visit *https://www.KallistiPublishing.com/report-a-typo/*.

DESIGNED IN THE UNITED STATES

CONTENTS

To my Mom, who taught me everything and provided constant and loving light amidst all the darkness.

To my wife, whose kindness and endless love nourishes and sustains me each and every day.

INTRODUCTION

ACHILLES, IN HOMER'S ILIAD, is the most fearsome warrior. He is the son of Thetis, a sea nymph known as a goddess of water. After Achilles is born, Thetis wants to make him invincible. Since he is half human, he is not invincible. So, she dips him into the sea holding him by the heel.

This act makes Achilles invincible everywhere except for where she was holding him to dip him in the water: his heel. Since that is the only part that did not get enveloped by the water, that is the only place he is vulnerable. The Trojans eventually are able to kill Achilles by learning this. Paris, a week and cowardly warrior, kills the mighty Achilles, the greatest of all of the warriors, by shooting an arrow through his heel.

So, too, can you shoot an "arrow" through the heels of your ailments. You may not be able to destroy your ailments, but by learning how to work around them, you are wounding them. You are rendering your ailments ineffective at disabling you.

To achieve this, you can become like another Greek mythological character: Antaeus. Antaeus is good at taking a beating. He is, unlike any modern hero, able to gain his strength by being defeated. Being thrown to the ground makes Antaeus stronger. Adversity is, then, his strength.

This idea is the very keystone of what is needed if you are going to shed the shackles of your nightmares. His particular importance hinges on the idea of strength through adversity. There are very few examples of this anywhere else in modern culture or modern literature. Characters having this quality are exceedingly rare. And it is this quality — and primarily this quality — that can free us — at least mentally — from the bonds of our disabilities.

There are certain assets that are required in addition to just being able to overcome being thrown to the ground. That is where Odysseus comes in.

In addition to becoming Antaeus, you'll need at least a hint of Odysseus. Odysseus is the legendary King of Ithaca in Greek myth. He is the protagonist of *The Odyssey*. He is known for his cunning as he is able to circumvent almost every instance of impending doom due to his brilliance. His asset is the power of his mind. Like Antaeus, this trait is also antithetical to most Western heroes in literature and culture today.

If you combine the story of Antaeus and the story of Odysseus, you have the essence of my argument toward overcoming adversity. This adversity may come in the form of mental illness, physical disability, oppression, economic struggles, or a wide variety of other human sufferings.

Antaeus is the starting point: he gives you the ability to keep getting up off the mat and to begin learning from your pain.

Odysseus gives us the tools: he shows you that you can find ways to think around your suffering in order to live a much more bearable life.

Finally, Achilles shows you that even though it may seem impossible, you can defeat whatever is in front of you.

"The sky is the limit, but most people with your injury won't be able to work in a box factory," one neuro-psychiatrist told me. He didn't know it then, but this statement was used over and over as motivation.

After my brain injury, most of my time was spent reading. That is, reading was my number one leisure activity in the days it seemed like physical therapy consumed every moment. The crushing depressions made this next to impossible at times, but there was no quitting.

Ernest Hemingway wrote an entire book about bullfighting. He described picadors at length. Picadors ride a horse in the arena with the bull. They carry a lance — a spear — and periodically and brutally jam it into the bull's neck in order to weaken it for the bullfighter.

I came to view my disabilities — mental illnesses, brain injury, and back pain — as similar wounds to those that picadors inflict on the bull. Hemingway wrote, "The world breaks everyone and afterward many are strong at the broken places. But those that will not break it kills. It kills the very good and the very gentle and a very brave impartially. If you are none of these you can be sure that it will kill you too but there will be no special hurry."

If the "picadors" of suffering in life were going to break me, then I could learn from how they broke me. If I could learn and understand "how" I was being broken, then I could devise a method or a way to work around almost any issue.

And that's what was done. This is the method I used then personally and a method I use now professionally to help others who have disabilities or other problems in social work. This method can apply to virtually any problem. Almost all problems have the same mechanism. A severe enough problem can either break you and destroy you or it can break you and you can learn from it. Hemingway was right.

Perhaps most importantly, there is no point in giving up. To surrender to any problem is to let that problem destroy you. It is unacceptable and it is simply a dead-end path. There is also no point in believing you will wake up one day and not have any problems. You probably always will, barring some great medical breakthrough or some miracle. It is unrealistic, then, to pretend they will vanish.

Your greatest asset, like that of Odysseus, is your mind. It is the ability to learn from your problems. By accepting your problems and then learning from them and really studying them and knowing yourself, you can work around them. This is the most realistic and pragmatic solution and ought to be sought in all cases where a cure is not likely.

My method will take a different form in everyone. It will make everyone who uses it stronger in one way or another. But it is important to remember that the most important ingredient is humility. You have to have the strength be able to fall flat on your face and let others see it. You have to be willing to openly acknowledge that you are not perfect. You have to strive to dismiss your pride and take refuge in introversion. It became clear early on that without humility, I have nothing. There is no true human growth in the absence of humility. The proud and the arrogant never really grow. Pride is almost always a problem. Humility always trumps pride. Unless pride is forgotten, there is little growth.

Whether you are in the doldrums of depression, the false world of psychosis, the desperation of poverty, the helplessness of oppression, the perils of physical pain, or suffer something — anything — on a daily basis, this book was written to give you at least modicum of hope. The formula that I will present in the following pages enabled me to overcome and transcend what virtually every medical professional said could not be transcended.

I did it by becoming more humble.

I did it by using my strengths.

I did it by becoming like Antaeus.

And in whatever way you are able, you can become like Antaeus, too.

VICTORY IN EVERY FALL

I

BIPOLAR DISORDER

THE SINGLE BARREL OF my shotgun had a metallic taste in my mouth. I sat in a blue reclining chair in my apartment. I angled the loaded shotgun into my mouth with its butt on the floor. Tears welled up and streamed down my face as I flirted with the very unpleasant possibility of the next life: the eternal nothingness or the unthinkable horror. The shotgun was angled to be certain that the blast would hit my brainstem so there would be nothing left of what I saw as my torture chamber.

About four years before this moment, I began to constantly practice how to commit suicide. Dad was approached during one of my horrific downs.

"Can you buy me a shotgun?" I asked Dad at twenty years old. I was incapable of getting one when I was depressed. That was a mammoth task that contained unthinkable social anxiety.

"Of course, son," Dad said eagerly. He loved guns and was thrilled with the prospect of his son wielding a shotgun. He was a former Marine who treated gun ownership with all the same necessity as the need for running water.

Dad got the gun and the gun meant freedom because it meant the ability to cease my life. It was gotten with one purpose: to know that there was escape to the prison of this world by destroying the prison of my brain at any given time.

This was a common occurrence in the bipolar depressions. They began at around age fifteen. By age twenty-four, they took up about eight months of my life most years. They are all-consuming and utterly paralyzing. There were only two things that ever stopped me from pulling that trigger and enabling the shotgun shell to blow apart my brain. The first is family, especially, my little Italian Mom. She dedicated her life to her kids and I did not spend a day in the doldrums of despair without Mom comforting in some way. In fact, she was the sole comfort most of the severe depressions. Her presence was the greatest deterrent of suicide. I knew this battle must be fought for as long as possible, if for no other reason than for her.

The second reason that metal trigger was never pulled was the fear of hell. The popular renditions of hell, while having little to do with Christianity, were terrifying. I read the Bible and studied it greatly. There wasn't anything like the popular depictions of hell. *But what if*, I thought, *what if the everlasting burning is the case?* The obsession with the idea and the fear of hell haunted this tortured mind day and night. It was the only thing I could imagine worse than this nightmarish existence. My brain went so far as to make me "feel" like I was burning when lying at night. The fear of hell was terrifying and was the second main factor stopping the pulling of the trigger and sending that shotgun shell full of pellets through my brain.

Bipolar disorder was a remarkably major giant to battle. It was like a plague on a daily basis for two-thirds of the year. The other third was like living in heaven on earth. The plagues are called depression and the heaven is called *hypomania* or *mania*. The cycles, as I will refer to them, did not come on all at once though. They transformed over time.

Around age fifteen, I began to have incredible difficulty sleeping. There was an utter exhaustion that descended on my consciousness all day, as if sleepwalking through life. This was in large part because at night, every night, I woke up and became filled with what felt like an electric current that gave boundless energy and made it impossible to sleep.

My days in ninth and tenth grade generally followed the same familiar pattern. At night, electricity would possess my body. Consciousness became very happy and giggly and, above all, productive. The days were filled with reading, writing, emailing and doing extensive research.

Dad worked as a welder on the railroad and drove an hour to work each day. He awoke at five in the morning. That meant that I was pretending to sleep around 4:45 AM. The alarm went off for school around 6:45 to 7 AM. I lay down and sometimes was able to fall asleep. Then, it was off to school. When sleep occurred, the electricity was gone as soon as my eyes opened. If I didn't sleep, it just petered out.

School was a nightmarish, awkward, socially anxious corridor that I had to walk through on a daily basis. I did well both socially and academically, but it was truly a struggle socially. There was a cognitive and social haze to fight through until returning home and the electricity could turn on again. Then there was a prompt passing out from exhaustion on the couch with Mom not too far away.

"You're always exhausted honey," she'd say.

"Yeah, Ma, it seems like it's a longer school day than seven hours. It's like an eternity."

It would be a few years from this point before telling Mom. I had no idea that anything was wrong with me — it was normal teenage stuff. There was no real baseline of what was "normal." And guys don't generally ask each other in high school, "Do you have trouble sleeping at night?" and "Do you feel like crap during the day?"

It was the time lying on the couch after school that I would get two or three hours of sleep throughout my high school career. Then came homework upon waking and by that time the electricity would return.

This was how the vast majority of days went from ages fifteen through seventeen. This is called *ultradian cycling*, which essentially means that both depression and mania are occurring within one day. There was no cognizance as to what was occurring early on. It was just me.

From ages seventeen through nineteen, the cycles lengthened. The electricity still came at night often times, but there was no more exhaustion or being in a fog in the morning at school. There were incredible feelings now both at night and all day. This would go on for a week or two. And then, it would turn off. I would gradually feel incredibly poorly for three weeks. Sleep was so easy and so attractive during these periods. Everything would slow down and all confidence would vanish. Eating would occur very little.

And obsessions. Oh, what obsessions! Bipolar disorder can carry with it severe obsessive ruminations as well. Suffice it to say, as a psychotherapist did, that I have "a bear of an obsession."

The time frame for the cycles grew from several days to several weeks. The symptoms grew stronger. Cognition became more arduous in the downs. Everything was clear and easy cognitively in the ups, or hypomanias.

During the hypomanias, I could solve all of the world's problems, become the next great novelist, and head the next great rock band. There were no problems. In the downs, or depressions, there was not even enough concentration to read a book.

Self-consciousness, self-hate, and social phobia became the norm. Losing weight occurred rapidly because food tasted metallic to me. Any interest in any project that Dr. Jekyll had, as I called the hypomanic version of me, was abandoned. There are memories of Dr. Jekyll getting into sports leagues online, card games, and many other things, satisfied that the enrollment would help Mr. Hyde have something to get him through the downs. It never did. An anxious Mr. Hyde would quit everything every time. Then, he would feel ashamed and humiliated that he did.

Somewhere in the body's transition from ultradian cycling to rapid cycling, there was a loss of capacity to cope with this new giant. This new giant was throwing me to the ground with a fury. At this point, there was no clear way to approach it. Up to this point in life, there was a conscious resistance to the drugs and alcohol in which others were losing themselves. As the nascent nightmare of bipolar disorder grew, anything was sought that would stop the depression-heavy bipolar disorder from tossing me to the ground for weeks on end.

And then alcohol entered. Alcohol seemed liberating to the emotional pain of bipolar disorder. This initially felt like my medication. So drinking occurred, and occurred heavily.

My bipolar disorder, at this point in time, could have been classified as bipolar II. There were severe depressions with hypomania, which is just below the destructive mania. The depressions and the hypomania just lasted very short times. Hypomania essentially means there was a period of feeling very well and extremely happy, but not so well and not so happy that it contained spending sprees, yelling in public, and other destructive behaviors that often come with full blown mania. There was still rapid cycling, which means the cycles changed every few weeks or months.

The alcohol consumption, to my sixteen-year-old

mind, seemed a perfect remedy. It "covered over" terrible feelings and, best of all, it blocked out most of the thoughts. At the time, it was the best remedy I tried — and so it was tried often.

In reality, alcohol was the worst remedy. The short-term benefits of it were the only benefits. There was no way for me to know that alcohol could make everything worse for bipolar disorder in the long-term. But I would never see the long-term. The biggest miscalculation with alcohol was not seeing how vulnerable it left one in the presence of bad people. The fact that this was not seen would cost me untold suffering due to a severe brain injury. This altered life forever and became another giant, which will be covered later.

Between ages eighteen to twenty, the cycles lengthened to a point that they were "rapid cycling." Rapid cycling is having more than four cycles — mania and depression — during one year. Therefore, the horror of the downs and the ecstasy of the manias got longer and there were no more phases that lasted eight or twelve hours. What was worse is that the depressions, as a general rule, always lasted about twice as long as did the hypomanias. Each depression was pregnant with intense obsessive fears. For instance, because there was a history of grand mal seizures, there was an increased chance that a seizure could occur. My favorite substance in the world, at the time, was coffee because in the doldrums of depression the caffeine, if taken in at the perfect time, could sometimes provide a small jolt to cognition and mood.

However, since caffeine is a psychostimulant, it increased the chances of having this incredibly feared seizure. So every time it was imbibed, the rest of the day was spent waiting to go into remarkable convulsions. The thoughts of having a seizure while driving and the possibility of hurting somebody were especially horrifying. This obsession stayed until Effexor destroyed caffeine consumption altogether.

The rapid cycling developed into textbook, full-blown, bipolar II disorder. By age twenty the cycles were graphed and charted meticulously. The down cycles at first lasted around three months, then elongated to around six months, and then became eight months at a time. No cycle was the same and all of them lasted different lengths of time. There was no concept after a while of how long the feeling of being held under water lasted, which is a good analogy of what the depressions felt like. The inability to concentrate or remember things, intense social phobia, and constant obsessions sidelined everything. Obsession ruminations can be a major part of bipolar disorder. They were so severe that they were all consuming.

A major obsession at this time was being homeless. Helplessness characterized consciousness more than half of the year when depressed. I believed I had no capacity to hold a job even if it was possible to finish my bachelor's degree. There was an endless struggle to get a bachelor's degree because of the downs. Switching colleges for credits and taking tele-courses became the norm largely because of the bipolar symptoms — the social anxiety of the classes, inability to concentrate, and other symptoms were just too much.

Even if it was not possible to get a bachelor's degree, what could be done? No menial task seemed too complex during the depressions. There was — literally — a fog around everything done and everything thought. Conversations with Mom sounded like this:

"So then why even get the degree?" I asked, pleading not to have to do anymore work in the fog of my mind.

"Because the degree will help you have a good life," she would say kindly. "If you want to chop wood for a living, honey, I support you. However, just get this degree so that you don't have to if you don't want to."

"You're suggesting enduring all the suffering of attending these classes with my malfunctioning consciousness just so I can have an insurance plan?"

"Yes, and you will see why one day. I know it is hard, honey, but I cannot tell you how glad I am that I got my college degree. I just want you to have that. After that, it's up to you," she said in her ever-loving, sage-like, and wonderful tone.

So, the decision was to do everything possible to get that degree. The feared fates of either committing suicide or living homelessly would be further contemplated as the degree was completed.

Mom and Dad were thirty-six years older and even if the disorder could be overcome, the dependence on them would not be able to last forever. Therefore, homeless preparations were carefully made. Eating a strict regimen of Ramen noodles and tuna was instituted because they were cheap meals and surely I could beg for enough money to get three or four dollars a day to eat. There were plenty of local creeks and waterways with plentiful water for drinking and bathing. There were several bridges in the city and in the winter months homeless shelters could be utilized.

This was the obsession: a bipolar obsession that had one foot in reality and one foot in a masochistic and obsessive nightmare.

Volunteering enabled me to see other people who struggled to live. Going to the food pantry was very hard during the down cycles because of anxiety around people and not understanding what they were saying very well. This became another major obsession. Due to the cognitive issues that come with the depressions, everything began to seem like it was said by the teacher in Charlie Brown: "*Wa wa wa wa wa wa…*" This obsession plagued me throughout my college career. Nevertheless, the premise was that the social anxiety could be "conditioned" by going to the food pantry constantly. It couldn't.

However, there was a new friend there. There were never many friends through all of this. The friend at the food pantry, though, was zealous about the Bible and wanted to teach me.

"It is good work," I said to Matt in the little church building where the food pantry was held. It was small but sufficient. You could always hear the buzz of engines running past on the busy street outside. "It isn't fun, but it's meaningful. It's good."

"Yes, it is," Matt said with certainty. He had blonde hair and was almost a decade older than me. He was a hard worker, but had to hold an ice pack just below his stomach much of the time he worked. His suffering created empathy between us even when his suffering was unknown.

"However," he continued pointing to Jim, "Jim over there believes it is going to get him to heaven if he sits here two days a week and hands out food. But this isn't the way you get to heaven. If you are going to heaven, this is something that would just come automatically to you."

I nodded and thought Matt had a screw loose. He was a good person although he was extreme and his ideas were different. I resisted at first but finally relented because of a desire to cultivate a belief in some greater answer and believing it could be in that Book and in that Faith. Matt and I emailed back and forth every day for months about each book in the Bible. There were many times I struggled to get through it during the downs.

My faith was much further developed by Leo Tolstoy's translation of Scripture and I remain a pious Christian to this day. It didn't help bipolar disorder at all, but it gave meaning and purpose in life. This came at a cost. As noted earlier, bipolar disorder got a hold of the concept of hell early on in the New Testament. This would become an obsession that would be a plague over the next decade.

Part of severe depression is endless feelings of inadequacy. No matter how good a job was done, there was an empty feeling that nothing was ever done. Perpetual inadequacy abounded and everyone did everything better. Even vaguely competent people seemed like superwomen and supermen. Others seemed to understand everything, have tremendous abilities, and can pay attention forever. There were many memories of crying hysterically when going to the movies. Every theater-goer seemed able to understand everything. Amidst the inadequacy, everyone else seemed endlessly capable. Others seemed like they were a superior species.

No medical treatment was sought. There was no understanding of what it was. The thought was that this brain and this body were just different than that of other people.

However, due to another ailment, Depakote was prescribed for seizures. This pill was ingested for about two years. It is also used to treat bipolar disorder in many people. During the two years on Depakote, life was like experiencing one long, hideous, nightmare. Depakote robbed hypomania, which was the only crack of biological hope in my mental health at this point. On Depakote, there was no feeling well — there was only the darkness.

After a short while, the hypomania was forgotten as if it never existed. Each horrible day was endured with Mom and faith that one day it would end. It was so bad that even lying in bed in the morning was an impossible task because the obsessions about hell and Mom and Dad being old and many other obsessions gave a feeling that one can't stand being in one's own skin. The medication created perpetual depression that sapped all of the little energy there was to get through each and every horrific day.

After this discovery, Depakote was slowly tapered off. This was against the doctor's advice. This was only one of two times the doctor's advice went unheeded. Within a few weeks, the electricity flooded back into consciousness and it seemed stronger and more divinely wonderful than ever before.

Then one day, my formerly depressed figure came barreling through the front door to see Mom.

"Everything feels so good! Everything is comprehensible! My memory is so much better and all concentration is back!"

Life for a few months became utterly exclamatory. Confidence returned. Thought returned. Memory was still very poor but nothing like it was when down. It was as if anything was possible and I was so capable and needed no periods or to stop at anything because life was one continuous circuitous loop and everything in the world felt like it was mine and I felt so much stronger for my suffering and could do anything.

That really was what it was like. Liberation. The façade of freedom returned and it was clearly all the medications fault and the whole thing was figured out.

But nothing was figured out. After a few months of the electric current animating my limbs, the electric current faded and disappeared. Mr. Hyde returned again and the world turned into a hateful and terrifying place. The mind slowed and memory disappeared.

It was at this juncture after being lifted up and thrown down for five years that a logical assumption was made. If Depakote could keep the electricity from coming, then maybe there was a drug that could keep "the horror" from coming, which is a term borrowed from *Heart of Darkness* and used to describe the downs. It is very fitting.

And so began the experimentation. A psychiatrist was called. The symptoms were described and a diagnosis came immediately. Anticonvulsant after anticonvulsant was prescribed to treat the bipolar disorder. These drugs are anti-seizure drugs. Depakote is in the same class of drug. Anti-seizure drugs have been proven to be effective in altering the cycles of bipolar disorder. What no doctor said, though, is that almost all of them are extremely good at taking away the electricity. Similarly, almost all of them are not particularly effective at destroying the depression. However, the belief the doctors conveyed was that if you limit the mania, you will limit the depressions. One doctor described it this way: "Your brain follows the Newtonian laws of science," he said with a smirk. "What goes up, must come down. If you stop it from going up, it won't come down." He said this very confidently.

This reasoning sounded fair to me. So I listened to him. And he was wrong. Every anticonvulsant medication — except Lamictal — just added new problems and side effects on top of crushing, suicidal downs. Each medication gave hope and then created more hopelessness than ever before.

Still, there was lots of reading. Reading provided much of the needed help. Many, many books on bipolar disorder were read voraciously. In a way, the reading was for my very existence because it was being done for self-preservation. There is no control with bipolar disorder as there is with many other maladies. There is no action on my part that is enabling it to do what it does.

One book that helped quite a bit was *The Bell Jar* by Sylvia Plath. She does not name her disorder because she wrote at a time when it was not well known. *The Bell Jar* chronicles her mental illness. In it she writes,

> *Wherever I sat — on the dock of the ship or at a street café in Paris or Bangkok — I would be sitting under the same glass bell jar, stewing in my own sour air.*

This was the same for me. I felt a kinship with Plath because she described a different version of the same illness. This helped and, although it was not a treatment, it was an empathic connection with another human being. It helped a lot.

But more than an empathic connection was needed. Answers and ways to avoid the horror were imperative. A book that gave some answers was *The Bipolar Handbook: Real-Life Questions with Up-To-Date Answers* by Dr. Wes Burgess. In this book, Dr. Burgess poses questions about bipolar disorder and he answers them. It was tremendously helpful and served as a wellspring of advice for treatments.

No book, however, gave a way of thinking about bipolar disorder that would enable combating it. Nothing worked. Existence became a petri dish in which changing sleep cycles, eating specific nutrients, and constantly adding and subtracting supplements and drugs to alter moods.

But nothing worked. It was, in Mr. Hyde's view, an untreatable giant. To Dr. Jekyll, the depressions were thought to be beatable in the beginning, but as the years went on Dr. Jekyll just blocked the depressions out as best he could because the depressions could not be overcome. It just became a hell to be dragged off into every few months. I remained there for an indeterminable amount of time and there was nothing to do about it.

A common analogy made in manias came from Dr. Faustus in Goethe's famous book, *Faust.* Consciousness was filled with short periods of joy and would then be dragged down to hell again and again and again. It was truly being thrown to the ground over and over and over. And there was no way of combating it.

The cycles, despite the pills, lengthened. They were now lasting much longer. The depressions lasted six to seven months at a time. The manias lasted three to four months at a time. It was hideous. Each day of the depressions was very different yet incredibly similar.

Sleeping as late as the body would allow seemed comforting. If sleep could last ten hours, there were only fourteen hours to get through till sleep could occur again. Sleep was by far the greatest activity to a depressed consciousness; that is, until reading that it exacerbates the depressions. For many years in the beginning, sleeping was a way to avoid it.

Did you know there is a point after which your body will not allow you to sleep anymore? When this point is hit, your body begins to hurt from lying in the bed. But there is still trepidation about getting up due to fear of the day. However, immediately upon waking, the thoughts began. The obsessions came flooding in with all their fury. Homelessness, hell, torture, what have you. The obsessions changed regularly, but what unified them was that all of them were based on fear. For example, there is a scene in the movie *Apocolypto* where there is a human sacrifice. It has been a full decade since I have seen that movie. But the sacrificing scene has never been forgotten. For many months it was obsessed on upon waking. It was as if it was being done over and over and over to my own body. The obsessions always force getting up.

Then each and every day came like a cruel freight train and ran me over. Each down day moved along with painful slowness and was an eternity unto itself. Mom remained my rock and she was always around. She helped distract from the obsessions and showed all the kindness in the world. Without her, I would definitely have killed myself. She was everything.

Despite her presence, though, there was no interest in anything. The news was watched but not understood. Reading was attempted but remembering what was read was incredibly difficult. Everything looked like it was surrounded by an intangible fog. Food tasted like metal and there was never a feeling of being hungry. As little as twenty and as many as sixty pounds were lost every down cycle. I was constantly and relentlessly thrown to the ground.

Furthermore, every decision seemed to be on the level of importance of launching a nuclear bomb. Making decisions was simply impossible and the indecision was paralyzing. Deciding what to eat or what to wear was unbearable.

Everything was unbearable.

All that could be thought about besides the obsessions was how to end consciousness. Suicide was the only rational decision. Nothing was helping: the medications, herbal supplements, the talking, doctors, and lifestyle changes all attempted different avenues at altering the wiring in an unwired brain. It seemed rational that destroying the very organ that served as a torture chamber was the only thing that would certainly work.

Every day was terrifying. Employment seemed even more impossible and so at this point every day was a battle to do schoolwork and to simply navigate the horrors of my own mind. There was no feeling in anything and there was no escaping in anything. At this point, each depression lasted more than half a year. It was unbearable.

But at the very moment that suicide was imminent, the electricity returned. It had a way of coming when there was a date on the calendar to commit suicide. And the electricity always changed everything.

Hypomania and mania are simply incredible. Whereas depression feels like you are drowning, hypomania feels like a jolt of electricity that hits you at night when you suddenly feel like you can leap tall buildings in a single bound. Then, in the morning, with rapid cycling, was like being drowned again. When the switch started to flip, it was like emerging from underwater, getting one breath in, and then being pushed back underwater in the morning and throughout the day.

There was never certainty if the electric circuits in the brain were flipping or not. In many down cycles this jolt would come once in a while but then would vanish and would immediately stay gone. I engaged in endless prayer. And there was no talking about it for fear that if it was said aloud, the electricity would not come. It was the feeling one has when trying not to disturb a bird that has landed nearby.

It would always, however, come. Consciousness would rock back and forth, getting jolts of the electricity at night for a few nights or for a week. Then, it would surge. It would spill over into the day and all of existence would be gloriously transformed. It felt like a switch was turned on and that switch changed my body entirely. It genuinely felt like an electric current, which is the closest analogy to it. It circulated throughout my body and the feelings that it gave were those of invincibility, greatness, and wholeness. Connections were made between everything. Thoughts were fluid and malleable and there was total control over them. All of the delusions that I was submerged in for all the depressed months evaporated overnight. Energy was endless and sleep was impossible except for two or three hours each night, if that.

It is the closest thing to heaven imaginable. Dr. Jekyll took over now and every time the electric current circulated his limbs it was obvious that Mr. Hyde — the depressions — would never return. Or, if they did, I'd be able to handle them the next time.

College became simple during the hypomanias. Speaking in every class was easy and it came to the point where Dr. Jekyll's voice was very often the dominant voice outside of the professor's voice. The invisible fear of social phobia no longer existed, although making friends was still a great struggle. I wrote zealously and many books were written during hypomanic episodes. Perfect grades were the norm. There were all kinds of activities and commitments agreed to that were ultimately retracted once the doldrums of depression returned. Regardless of whatever was thought, that thought would come immutably and inevitably and perfectly. There always would be an inevitable return to the depths of depression that would destroy all that was built in the hypomania.

"Hey Kurt," Jeff would say to me. Jeff was tall and had brown hair. He had deep brown eyes that made them appear black. He grew up down the road and we were friends since kindergarten. "My family has a card game coming up this weekend and we need another dealer. Can you do it?"

"Sure," I said, elated to be social. The card game was a month down the road. By the time it came around, Mr. Hyde had taken over my body. Jeff was called with tear-filled eyes.

"I'm so sorry, Jeff. I feel so embarrassed and humiliated, but really cannot do it. I feel too confused and terrible. It's those depressions we talked about."

Almost every social interaction went that way. It didn't take long to lose any relationship.

I read extensively. With Mom by my side, we would read and find what to try next and what to do. After years of always going back into the depressions, no matter how good or long lasting the high was, it was clear from a rational standpoint that the low was coming back. We plotted new strategies and treatment to see if we could curb the severity of the next depression.

In the end, however, nothing worked.

The anticonvulsants only took away mania.

The herbal supplements — the endless herbal supplements! — were perfectly useless.

We would measure out vitamins and nutrients we read about — from B-1 to folic acid — and carefully measured amounts were taken. No benefit.

The best treatments were knowledge and empathy. The books enabled understanding of this enormous giant. Bipolar disorder is different in every person, but the broad similarities are remarkable. How it generally works, what exacerbates it (like too much sleep), what treatments there are, were all read about veraciously and understood. This was incredible knowledge, but reading did not stop bipolar disorder from slamming, holding, and taking life hostage for more than half of each year.

The empathy always came almost exclusively from

Mom. She remained during every moment of the horror. We talked about it every day and it was her empathy, her kindness, and her genuine connection that served as a veritable life raft that I needed to cling to in order to endure the slings and arrows of bipolar pain. That is truly the only strategy, in the end, that was rational: *to endure.*

The giant of bipolar is utterly unlike many other maladies. There was not a clear mindset or strategy that worked. Bipolar disorder virtually made me into two people — and nothing that helped one helped the other. There was no behavior or mindset that could stop the life from going out of me so that I was not reduced to a tortured and helpless blob for two thirds of the year. Learning to appear proficient — to fake understanding or recalling things during the downs — became a great and necessary act.

But it was only that: fake. Faking something does not take any of the pain away. The suffering of bipolar disorder seemed to have no exit. Enduring it forever was not an option and ultimately the fear of suicide was inescapable. There was no other option but to try to hang on for as long as possible. I would beg for God's forgiveness when it finally had to be done.

Since there is no behavioral solution and since the electric current is purely biological, my deduction was that the only real permanent solution was in chemical form. But medications continued to fail me. Time and options were running out.

The most influential literature to me at this time — twenty-three to twenty-four years old — was existential literature such as that of Camus and Sartre and Tolstoy's translation of the Bible. Those philosophical stances combined to give a sense of purpose in life. Happiness is not the goal of life. Rather, the goals, for me, became to do one's moral duty and have purpose. This purpose was personal and mine was to transform this life into a sacrifice for the well-being of other people. This made meaning. After volunteering at a food pantry and an economic organization that helped people keep their heat on, it was confirmed.

My thesis was simple:

> *I cannot beat this and got a "bum life." It will be used to help others and will seek out death as quickly as possible along the way. Poor lifestyle habits will hasten the decay of this body in all ways so that death may be hastened.*

There was not much that could be done to help others in what was my present form. Credentials had to be acquired. So, it was off to social work graduate school.

There were two graduate colleges in the area: Marywood, which was about forty minutes down the road, and Binghamton, which was about an hour and a half away and over the border from Pennsylvania into New York. However, I never tried leaving home. It was hypothesized that a new environment could be beneficial from a mental health standpoint. The cost of Binghamton, a state school, was far cheaper than Marywood, a private school. It seemed like a bad move, but something environmental needed to be tried. Binghamton opened the door to admission and the plan was to be back with Mom every weekend. This was a desperate attempt at a solution.

Focusing on helping someone else and making meaning of life was more effective than most other strategies. However, it was no cure-all. Misery now had meaning, though.

However, the cycles, unexpectedly, did not change at all in Binghamton. Furthermore, the cycles became worse because there was no support or comfort, especially in the most desperate moments.

Furthermore, Mom was a social phobic. Therefore, she did not come up more than twice the entire time Binghamton was my home. This meant the best coping mechanism could only be utilized on the weekends. This added immensely to the stress.

Reading voraciously and going to doctors became the major coping mechanisms. I did not, however, get better. Rather, I deteriorated. This giant was too big and it felt like it could not be beaten at all. There was daily consolation in the single barrel shotgun with which suicide was practiced.

What is, perhaps, the most disheartening aspect of bipolar disorder is the utter lack of treatments. Broadly, there are only two: medical and nonmedical. Medical treatments include pills, which are, by far the most common treatment. That route was believed to be exhausted. Antidepressants, anticonvulsants, and a third category, antipsychotics were all tried. Several medications were tried from each class. Medications were combined. Nothing worked.

Other medical treatments include transcranial magnetic stimulation. This is the doctor essentially putting a magnet to your head in hopes that the current the magnet induces may have a positive effect on your neurotransmitters. At the time, there was little evidence at all for the efficacy of this. There was little interest in experimenting in this because there was little known about it at the time.

The medical route also offered ECT — electroconvulsive therapy. This is the big daddy of treatments. The premise is simple: the doctors strap you down and send electricity through your brain so you have a seizure. Seizures can improve depression, miraculously at times. ECT was always heralded as an effective treatment. It universally has a terrible effect on memory. Ernest Hemingway said that ECT was, "ruining my head and erasing my memory." There was fear of having more seizures. One seizure was had in the past and once you have another, they can become recurrent. So, ECT was out.

Lastly, there was vagus nerve stimulation. This is the surgical installation of an electrical device near the vagus nerve. It pulsates and that stimulation is supposed to help the cycles. There was little evidence that this is truly effective and the concept of being a guinea pig was not a pleasant one.

That was it. When broken down, it seemed a hopeless array of treatments. Pills almost universally hurt more than they helped at this point. Transcranial magnetic stimulation and vagus nerve stimulation seemed like pie-in-the-sky treatments without much to back them in terms of evidence. And ECT was just plain horrifying.

So, I ran with open arms to nonmedical treatments to beat this Goliath that was destroying my existence by throwing me to the ground each and every day. First among these were the nonmedical pills: vitamins, supplements, and so on. Supplements consumed included a B-complex, folic acid, and pretty much every vitamin known to man that the literature stated could have an impact of bipolar disorder. Tryptophan, the precursor to serotonin, was said to be beneficial to mood and it was taken daily. A supplement called 5-HTP was taken after reading a book on it. Therapeutic "trials" were given to everything. Each supplement was taken for more than a month. Each was journaled. Each was charted. But nothing. Not a single one was helpful. They did not hurt, though.

Light therapy was another nonmedical treatment. A light box was purchased — a large, rectangular box that shines very bright light. It is supposed to simulate sunlight. The sunlight is said to raise neurotransmitters and lift moods, as it does in every living human being. I stared into it for long periods each day. It was on while reading, while eating cereal for breakfast, and while watching TV. But there was no effect.

At age twenty-nine, after suffering with bipolar disorder for about fourteen years, psychotherapy was fervently tried. It was tried at least once per week for almost two years. And it was helpful, though it did not cure the Jekyll and Hyde existence. There were not many tools attained to help minimize the pain of bipolar disorder, either. What psychotherapy for bipolar disorder did, however, was give me another human connection from someone who understood the madness of it to some extent. I had Mom. However, she was not privy to the literature and could not validate the disorder beyond a certain point. The psychotherapist, a social worker, could — and did. It was a small crutch. The therapist provided empathy. This increasingly scarce human resource is one of the most potent and effective treatments for bipolar disorder. The psychotherapist gave empathy from someone other than Mom. That was invaluable in itself.

"Simple pleasures," he would say as he drank a cup of tea in the small, crowded office in Ithaca. "What you are describing are simple pleasures. They seem to be getting you through the down days of your bipolar disorder."

"Simple pleasures?"

He took a deep breath. "You said you like three cigarettes a day. You said you look forward to each one immensely. You have one on the drive home from work and two at night. You have created a simple pleasure. You have to do this across the board: find many simple pleasures."

"You mean anything like this would do?"

"Of course," he said before drinking the flavored tea that he held with both hands. "You cannot stop the pain and horror of your depressions. However, you can create things to look forward to that will help you endure them."

This was, perhaps, the best advice that the therapist gave regarding the treatment and management of bipolar disorder. It was used extensively. All types of little pleasures served as a carrot at the end of the stick to keep getting up off the ground and moving forward each painful day.

Nevertheless, amidst all of his nonmedical treatments, none were truly helpful at eliminating the pain and torment of bipolar disorder. This was obvious. The emergency became to figure out some sort of new treatment or different lifestyle. Because each down became more intolerable in its own right, each was wearing down my capacity to weather the storm. Paradoxically, I grew tougher for enduring each cycle yet grew diminished because each cycle took so much life out of me. Suicide continued to hover over and haunt me.

Reading and writing, as with OCD, were by far the best therapies for me. I wrote every day. First, writing was in a daily journal. This gave a canvas for my rage and disgust and other feelings. It was and is to this day the best nonmedical treatment. It enabled the description of problems to an invisible audience that seemed to listen and care. Writing enabled the validation of the nightmare. It helped — and continues to help — enabling memory of what was tried and not tried. The daily fight to get through day after day of the torturous thoughts and atmosphere were codified by writing and that codification ensured that all that suffering was not being done in vain. There is no way to fully express the wonderfulness that writing was in my life or the meaning that it brought. It even gave a sense of community, as so many authors, such as Hemingway or Plath, talked about suffering maladies similar to mine.

Reading was similarly effective. The issue with reading was that during the depressions, concentration was so arduous that reading became impossible. During these times, everything was slow and languid and there was no memory of what was just read and in my brain the obsessions constantly asked the question, *How are you understanding the written word?* After a while, everything on the page was stumbled over. The inability to concentrate, the incredibly poor memory in the depressions, and the thick, almost palpable mental fog truly made it impossible to read and especially to recall what was read. But when focus was possible and enabled reading, reading was very therapeutic. I always read and reading has always served to be one of my greatest strengths. It, in particular, gave a form of the community that was longed for. There is a certain camaraderie that is created when the author has suffered something similar. These connections became great consolations. Through my authors, there was a perceived community — even if they were not alive.

In addition to reading and writing, loved ones were

the other great treatment who helped though the full eighteen years of the nightmarish manic-depressive cycles. They were always near and the impact of this care and concern is immense. In those years, Mom pushed me, ever warmly, to always continue. If I am anything, I owe her everything. When there was no way to concentrate or see through the fog, loved ones gave some modicum of focus. Mom gave both the drive and the compassion that was needed to press on in my daily battle. Without this, the depths of depression are often too dark and suicide seems inevitable. She and my wife were and are always the lights amidst all the darkness of my mind. They always empowered me to get up off the ground when bipolar threw me down.

But they were far from a cure-all. Despite the existence of loved ones and writing and reading, the biological inevitability of the depressions deepened. Each depression felt more intolerable than the last. There was a feeling of unrewarded accomplishment for suffering with a severe depression sentence for eight months only to serve the next depression sentence after a brief break for nine months. I always got manic again and ate all of the weight back. There were always new plans to do all kinds of great things followed by an abrupt departure and plenty of humiliation. But nothing seemed to stop this cycle of suffering.

For example, let's return to that fateful decision to go to graduate school in New York. To do that, all that I knew to be a coping mechanism had to be left — all my comforts in the current environment of home. In the mania, leaving all that seemed doable and everything would be okay because I could, of course, do anything. The depressive version of me thought it was idiotic and unwise. However, it was obvious to both manic and depressive selves that a new setting could change things and that there could be some truth to that. So, after getting an undergraduate degree, I took a leap of faith and applied to graduate school in New York. It was a full hour-and-a-half away from anything that created even a little comfort. The classes were difficult due to intense and awkward social anxiety. Also, repetitive studying and hard work were required to understand what was going on because of the thick fog that enveloped my mind. There were no acquaintances, friends, or loved ones in New York and Mom was not at the end of each painful day because she was over one hundred miles away. The move did not help the depressions and having a new setting made everything worse because it took away the person who comforted most.

Oftentimes, people say that a change of environment and a new world will fix a mental health problem. There is no doubt that this can help for some specific cases. And there is not a single regret for studying social work and attaining a LMSW. However, the move to New York was extremely foolish and made life far more difficult. Moving to a strange place without any of the few comforts that I did have was a horrible decision. Nevertheless, there is always a way to get back up off the ground yet again.

The giant of bipolar disorder was simply getting too

big. Getting through the day — from sleep to sleep — continued to be an unfathomable burden. Hikes were one of those simple pleasures and on those hikes the question that came to mind incessantly was, *Is it possible to endure fifty more years of this?* I asked this over and over in my journals as well.

It was in Binghamton that the decision was made to kill myself. The shotgun was ready to go. It was clear that it would obliterate my brain — and that was the goal. Any form of suicide that did not destroy the brain was simply unacceptable. The brain was the wellspring of this horrific reality and it needed to be annihilated. This ruled out hanging, drowning, suffocating, taking pills, and a long list of other possibilities. Blowing my head off with a shotgun was the only permissible way to take my own life.

I began practicing late at night. There were places — secret places — to practice putting the shotgun into my mouth and resting the butt on the floor. I angled the shotgun so that the barrel was pointed toward a specific part of the brain — a part that would leave this body with no possible hope for consciousness and would destroy the very parts in which science states my disorders reside. The cold of the metal barrel in my mouth always produced a metallic flavor. For some reason I was numb all the time and it was only then that the tears came. It was only then when realizing the magnitude of what I was going to do that the tears were allowed to roll forth.

Bipolar disorder carries with it a world of different moods. It is not just sadness and ecstasy. Each of the moods served as a looming giant over my crippled world. Existence was knocked down in one way or another by all moods, even hypomania, since it always got me into all of the things that I was terrified of when down. There certainly was sadness — was there ever sadness! But sadness does not dominate the feelings as many think it does. Terror does. Numbness does. But fear was the keystone of my bipolar disorder. It was the biggest giant and it remained a constant. Fear was prominent. There was also an overarching sense of numbness. In many of my journal entries, I used an analogy of being on a conveyor belt of torture. There was no exit from that conveyor belt. It was like being strapped down and forced to be on a ride. After a while, the terror continues to remain but you know what's coming and you just kind of become, in a sense, numb to it.

When I was over that barrel of that shotgun, though, the sadness was allowed to flow out of me. The tears came with it and I always remember my hands on the single barrel of metal being wet.

The shotgun was small enough that I could use my thumb to pull the trigger. Hemingway used the shotgun to kill himself. He used to rehearse it in front of his friend. He would put the butt of a rifle on the ground and press the two barrels into the roof of his mouth and would use his big toe on his right foot to pull the trigger. I was certainly no expert marksman like Hemingway and knew relatively little about guns. I was terrified that I would make a mistake by using a toe to pull the trigger. Therefore, I was able to find a shotgun that was small enough that the index finger could be used to pull the trigger.

Four or five months into every depressive cycle for close to a decade were spent practicing suicide. I pulled the trigger over and over and as terrifying as the sound was — the clicking noise of the shotgun hammer — that sound was equally as comforting. There were these terrifying reservations at all times, however. This was flirting with the eternal.

The first reservation about suicide was about Mom and then Tanya once we met and got married. They caused the tears. The action was likely to devastate them on a level the likes of which I could not handle. I recall the earlier years trying to prepare her for it.

"Ma, I don't know how much longer I can take these downs."

"I know, honey," she would say as she patted my head. "We have to find something for you that works."

"But if we don't, Mom, I am not positive how long I'll be able to take it. It's like riding a bull. It cannot be done forever."

"Well, all we can do is keep trying different things and hope something works for you," she said sweetly.

"Right. But if that's not possible, if it cannot be endured, Ma, you do know that you're the best Mom who ever lived and that never in a thousand lives could a better one have been given, right?"

"Thank you, honey," she would reply.

Suicide was alluded to but seldom directly spoken about. The Sunday nights before returning to New York when depressed were often spent crying hysterically. It seemed for certain to me that one of those times I left would be the last time I saw my Mom because of my impending suicide. One time we sat in the parking lot of Barnes & Noble. A very, very sad goodbye was said to Mom and it was absolutely heartbreaking to leave her because of how much I believed it would be the last time. It was primarily the thoughts of hell and the impact on her that I never pulled the trigger. Upon the visits to Pennsylvania several times per month, I made sure to squeeze her a little tighter due to the fear that I simply would be pushed over that edge and would never return once in New York.

Another reason for never pulling the trigger was my uncertainty as to where to aim the barrel. By this time, my knowledge of the brain was extremely proficient from having read so many books. There were obviously no instructions for how to do such a thing so reason was the only guide. Should the shell be aimed at the frontal lobe, the limbic system, or the brainstem in order to completely destroy the area that caused so much torment? The deep and abiding fear was that somehow there would be survival and somehow that survival would leave bipolar disorder intact. There was always great consolation in having that shotgun because I knew it could destroy consciousness. However, there was not absolute certainty that even it would work perfectly as desired and for such an enterprise there could be no error. Endless research was done. But the fear always lingered.

Another reason for having a Hamlet-like pause was facing the Eternal. In the best case scenario, after the trigger was pulled, there would be nothing after: no afterlife, no pain, no hope — and no fear. Nothingness. That was longed for desperately. No consciousness. Eternal oblivion. As appealing as it was — it is — for all of us, frightening. This is because the fear is biological. We are built biologically to survive. Therefore, death is innately fearful. This reality was obvious each and every time I sat in a little recliner or on the ground and angled the shotgun for the brainstem or frontal lobe or limbic system to enter into what hopefully was oblivion.

The final reason is an extension of the last. *What if it is not nothingness?* I thought. *What if it is worse — much worse? What if there is a hell?* This loathsome sentiment plagued this mind for years. These obsessions have, as their foundation, the belief that hell is infinitely worse than the now. Obsessions abounded on fire and actually "feeling" fire and realizing that nothing could be worse than feeling it constantly. These obsessions were haunting over the barrel of that gun. The fire was felt when I sat over it. Even the possibility of the pellets in that shotgun shell jettisoning this consciousness to an even more hideous existence ignited utter horror. Why shouldn't it? If so many treatments, like the awful Effexor or Seroquel, made this consciousness worse — far worse — why couldn't the remedy of suicide backfire too? Why couldn't there be an even worse place?

Still, suicide in one form or another was inevitable. Alcohol was now being used at least several days a week to get through the day. The rationalization was that God would possibly see drinking as just a slower version of the shotgun. It was comforting to put the shotgun in my mouth and know that all of this life's torture would theoretically stop if the trigger was pulled. It was done often as if it was a calming pacifier and it was the way my eventual end would most likely come. A promise to God that I would keep getting up as long as possible often propelled me forward.

As you can see, I did not feel like Antaeus with bipolar disorder at first. The reason is because there was no clear way to beat severe depression. I read and read about different ways to beat it. The extremely optimistic alter ego, the hypomanic Dr. Jekyll, always wrote to Mr. Hyde that he will "figure out a way" to keep Mr. Hyde from coming back all the time. But he never did. He couldn't. When the electricity ebbs away and the horrors of the depression come back, it paralyzes in every way. Severe depression always took over and always won.

Antaeus was illustrated by continuing to getting up after being pulled down into the doldrums of depression. Forging ahead by any means necessary was all that mattered. The struggle was immense. But I kept pushing forward. A lot of help was given. And it was accomplished.

I was Antaeus and that strength was gained in both

knowledge and experience. It was like a soldier being pushed into the dirt. No matter how impossible, the mission had to be finished. The mission was simply getting through this life in a moral way.

I wasn't Antaeus in that it seemed not to be beatable. Hypomania — Dr. Jekyll — believed it had thrown depression to the ground but it never did. It always came back. It seemed it could not be destroyed. All remedies failed. I routinely made jokes about getting a tattoo stating *ENDURE* across my back. Because that was truly all that could be done: enduring it.

Only one friend was made in graduate school. He was a very pleasant man who was older than me and grew up in same area. He wore glasses and was very bright and extremely energetic. Our Italian ancestors grew up in a tiny neighborhood in the same village and we often joked that we must be related. He is very kind man and we were paired together in one of our social work classes at graduate school. He said that he worked in social service… nothing more.

So when he asked me to come up and do an internship for the agency he worked for, it seemed like a great opportunity. This incredibly humble and good man ended up being one of the directors of that agency. It was disappointing to learn that this agency was thirty-even more miles from Mom and the comfort she gave. It made a total of about two-hours-and-fifteen minutes of driving distance from New York to Pennsylvania between his agency and Mom. But there was no other option. To succeed at employment, I needed someone kind and compassionate and empathetic. Very few social opportunities presented themselves and this was a quality human being who somehow saw potential. Therefore, it seemed a moral imperative to lay all of my cards on the table before going to do an internship for him.

"Before we go any further, I want to be completely honest with you." It was a cool January day in Binghamton. We were sitting in a small café and drinking beer.

"About what?" he asked and nodded for me to continue.

A deep breath was taken. "Well, you know I have problems. But I never told you how severe some of them can be. One of them absolutely destroys my life. It's bipolar disorder."

My friend smiled. "That explains a lot," he said, almost musing to himself. "I'm not too worried though, Kurt."

"You understand that I haven't had a job since high school due to all my problems?"

"It doesn't worry me," he said reflexively, "I've been doing this for twenty-four years. I have a pretty good handle on people. I see what you can do in class. You are incredibly prepared. Better than that, you're as bright as they come. You have every good intention in the world and genuinely want to help people. Yes, you have problems. But the rest will fall into place."

It was too good of an opportunity. And so began the beginning of one of the best treatments for bipolar – *employment.* I was twenty-five years old and about nine years after the ultradian cycling started. The prayer that a new setting and the inclusion and meaningfulness of employment would help beat the bipolar cycles dominated thought.

However, the internship was horrible at first. It let me see just how bad the social anxiety was. In fact, during the depressions, there was intense fear to go to the internship and each morning I found myself on my knees praying that each day would be easier than the last. Every effort was made to reason through the irrational oppressing web of social anxiety but nothing worked. Each day, Angelo, my friend and now supervisor, had me go to a group home for individuals who were suffering from severe and persistent mental illness, which you might call ironic. Other days, he took me around with him. Those days were great. However, the long days at the halfway house were torturous. No one was cruel, but the presence of other individuals suffering from mental illness and at least two counselors were the source of remarkable anxiety. I could not stand my own skin. There was no ability to tolerate sitting there and there was too much fog and confusion in my brain to know what was going on. Everything was incredibly awkward, everything said felt embarrassing, and most of the time was spent trying to go and solitarily do some project — trying to escape. Little was learned from it.

Amidst this anxiety, functioning was perceived as at least adequate. Writing newsletters for the agency was how any notoriety was gained despite the downs. Angelo, at the conclusion of the internship, offered a job. Self-perception rendered me incapable of doing much of anything considering how intensely uncomfortable others were to me and how confusing and overwhelming everything was. *Yes* was the answer to the job offer, however. *Yes* was said based on the ongoing hypothesis that if submerged in the social world long enough, all anxiety would go away, and cognition would not be so rushed and nervous.

The job was running a small program that moved furniture into the homes of people. The people the program assisted had severe and persistent mental illness, which at the time was often referred to as *SPMI* in New York State by their Office of Mental Health. It was terrifying and overwhelming. More hours were worked every day than were paid for because of the desire to do a good job. I was paid to do it three days per week but did everything so thoroughly and perfectly due to obsessions that it took more hours to get it done. The program owned a large pickup truck and that is where most of the time working was spent. It was filled with other people who struggled with mental illness and we worked together to move furniture into people's homes who needed it. I struggled because if they did not show up, the work still had to get done. Attendance can be a struggle at times for individuals suffering from severe mental health conditions. This had me lifting far too much. Confrontation in the downs was simply impossible and it was very difficult to tell the workers to do something if they did not want to do it. There was a true zeal to succeed at my first real job, however. And each and every day became filled with anxiety and terror and there was no pleasure in any of it. Of course, another down cycle descended when I started the job in October. The stress of the internship and the job kept me in a down cycle.

After work, there was a cold drive to Binghamton and to the tiny efficiency apartment that was called home. Each night, my muscles would tingle from overwork. Lifting so much furniture each day was a foreign activity and each night it felt like there were fire ants biting all of the muscles in my back and arms. Being there only three days per week and being too socially anxious to task the workers to do what I could not resulted in taking on too much work too fast.

It was a poor strategy. In four months, I ended up in the hospital. One day, my back just froze up while trying to type up a novel. It froze and there was no movement and it was off to the emergency room. To this day it really hurts — typing or standing for long causes great pain and numbness. This was yet another plague caused in large part by social anxiety, fear and confusion due to the giant of bipolar disorder.

Angelo offered another job when I quit due to my back. This job was running a new program for the agency. It was funded by New York State and it was an apartment program for individuals with chemical dependency issues and issues with homelessness.

This offer was a turning point in my life. Angelo stated that in the short time running the furniture program (nine months), it was impeccably done and many changes improved the program — and improved it a great deal. He said that he felt very confident and explained why I needed to run this new program.

"If I say yes to this job, then life will be completly relocated up there. This will alter my future. It is a big commitment, Mom," I said while pacing in our living room on a Saturday. The anxiety was debilitating. Uncertainty abounded. So the guidance was sought of the one whose guidance was always sought: Mom.

"It is, honey, but it is also an incredible opportunity. It is hard to pass up a job where you will get to work alone to help people. It really is a great opportunity."

"Are you saying you think I should do it?"

"I'm saying that it is your choice. I'm also saying that it is a great opportunity and one that would be hard to pass up."

My Mom was always accustomed to saying what she said now, "What do you have to lose?"

Everything was the first thought. There is no proof that a down cycle could be managed working and each down cycle took me to the brink of lost employment. There was no ability to stand for more than a few minutes without having to sit down from pain. There was no ability to extend my arms forward to type without strong pain shooting throughout the upper back. And to top it all off, the current drug being taken for bipolar disorder, Effexor, had caused my entire system to malfunction. Every time there was a social situation nausea consumed consciousness. There was always a small notebook in my pocket and copious notes were taken throughout each and every day. In short, every day was an invisible and constant battle that no one else could see. Every night, my prayers were for Mom and Dad and the world and all that — and also for death. Death was the only desire. Period. To me, suicide remained inevitable and thinking about it was the only relief outside of sleeping. The only real desire was to show God that everything possible was tried and given the best shot before that trigger was pulled.

Etched into memory was that day Mom and I discussed the job. She made it all sound so simple. If the job was tried and failed, I would just finish the master's degree and come home. She said it was "no problem."

However, the incessant and demanding daily pains — not understanding what was said by people, the endless lack of rest no matter how much sleep was gotten, the constant quagmire of shame entered into each day, the fact that there was no memory of anything anyone said, the daily nausea and angst that was so intense that finishing graduate school was very uncertain — these and many other problems that dominated thought each and every day were too much. It was a full-time job just to get through the day. But Mom thought it was a good idea.

And she was a sage. And all of life was so absurd anyway.

So I would do it. After all, Angelo was the boss and this is probably the best it would get. If this was failed, then failure probably lurked around every corner.

Albert Camus once said,

Without work all life goes rotten.

This quote was hung above my desk. Work, for all its horror, was the best treatment I found to date for my bipolar disorder. It distracted me from my own mind. It made time go by quicker. So, I would try it. But I resolved that if this was failed, there would be no point in finishing graduate school. There was only so much someone could take. If this failed, suicide was the next move on the chess board of life.

But there was no failure at the job. A tiny office that used to be a closet was set up in a fourteen-person halfway house. The closet served as both a jail cell and a sanctuary. The only time I spent out of the office was when it was absolutely necessary for the job, which was often, of course. During the manic cycles the door was left open and music blared so everyone in the house could hear. Every depression, the resignation papers were filled out and the nickname "The Ghost of Charles St." was given to me because the office door was closed all the time and I talked to no one and came and went without anyone noticing.

Every mania, the goal was to run all of the housing services at the agency after my supervisor retired. The manias were heaven and during them strong and ever-changing battle plans were made to fight the depressions. Each problem was partialized and every effort was made to minimize all of them. This was a better way to fight when off the ground rather than try to fight everything at once.

This is still the plan today. Copious techniques have been created for my memory to shield the fact that, as one neuropsychologist told me, "It is as poor as an old man's memory," especially when I am depressed. Sticky notes abound everywhere and memory aids that range from using regulating circadian rhythm to knowing when certain things are supposed to be done to looking deeply into people's eyes for any expression that indicates I already told them whatever it is I am saying. Because typing is an integral part of the job, the desk had a keyboard drawer that enabled my arms to be kept down near the knees while typing. And because that still sends remarkable pain through my back, Dragon software filled that void. Dragon software enables speaking to become typing… which saved the aforementioned job after the back pain started and it is also how this book is being typed.

There are so many tricks that can be utilize to overcome a disability. For every single problem — every single way I have been thrown to the ground — there is a trick to either avoid it, to defeat it, or to mask it.

You can create work-arounds and tricks to every single issue. These won't eliminate ailments but will enable a way to work around them. These workarounds do not necessarily deny suffering, but can empower you to be functional despite many disabilities.

This formula is true for most maladies. These work-arounds and tricks empowered me to work around the emotional and cognitive impacts of bipolar disorder and, most specifically, through the bipolar depressions. The manias were never a problem because most often they were hypomanias. Despite their efficacy, though, no matter how many tricks or strength based strategies were used for bipolar disorder, there were so many things that still seemed impossible to work around. For instance, there is no conceivable way to fake having energy when your body is lifeless and limp and all the sleep in the world has no effect. The world around you can be fooled that you can concentrate through a well-timed series of nods and statements like, "That makes sense," when concentration was impossible or you were struggling to understand what people were saying. But no trick or workaround, except for the distraction of work or meaningful activity, was ever effective at escaping the tyranny of my own thoughts.

To this day, work remains the best environment for my mental illness. Despite all of these pitfalls, work gave something that was previously not fully present: *work gave meaning*. Work continues to give meaning and this meaning enables the transcendence of the self. Meaning creates a world wherein there is less time to dwell on the self, due to the higher purpose it allows you to see. All the symptoms and problems are still there but there is no time to dwell on them or how terrible life is because of those symptoms. The importance of meaning and purpose cannot be overstressed in overcoming these giants. It is amongst the most effective treatments — not solutions, but treatments. It will never defeat the giants, but most times they cannot be defeated anyway. It will, however, enable you to circumvent the giant. And that makes all the difference.

In short, meaning makes suffering more bearable. Every night for almost fifteen years now, I can go to sleep knowing the world is a tiny bit better because of my existence. No matter how much I suffer, I know this to be an immutable fact. It is a blessing to feel satisfied knowing that everything that could be done was done and that, as Ralph Waldo Emerson is often attributed to having said,

> *To know even one life has breathed easier because you*
> *have lived*
> *This is to have succeeded.*

This is success and this also makes meaning for me.

The creation of one's own meaning or purpose is a profoundly effective psychological intervention. I found what makes meaning for me: *doing good for others.* It is, at the end of the day, what keeps me going. It is purpose and I have the passion and I learned that I have the passion and drive to do it no matter how much I am ailing.

No matter what your giant is, if you can find meaning in a philosophy or activity, if you can find purpose, it will help you transcend your malady. Your meaning will serve as your proverbial carrot that keeps you going and distracts you as you go through the endless drudgery of your problem. Introspection enables us to find our meaning. Socrates said, "Know thyself." Such advice must be taken very seriously.

Meaning in all its forms serve as major weapons against all my problems. However, there are an almost endless supply of other "tricks," strengths, strategies, etc. to circumvent the specific nightmares each one presents.

One major trick is *logic*. Psychoeducation revealed that bipolar disorder was very real, very cyclical, and that the stakes were life and death. It helped to reveal that this mind was sick and deceiving. The only choice was to wade through the deception with education.

With bipolar disorder depressions, the tricks that were used were not always successful. For instance, going downstairs in the halfway house and trying to interact with the staff and clients for a bit, knowing the shame and guilt that would be felt — the shame and guilt that made even eye contact incredibly difficult — was a lie. This was how the downs were endured and the techniques were helpful. But nevertheless, it was unendurable. Being social was like riding a wild bull. I could only do it for a few moments.

"Come downstairs, Kurt," Angelo said. He perceived socialization, even if it were forced, as the best remedy to the issue.

Walking downstairs caused trembling. Reason kept saying that there was nothing to fear. I can still remember the sweat on my hands and the terror and nervousness and shakiness. It was all irrational but it was real.

"Hi, what's going on?" I asked with a large wide

smile. The shame was invisible to them but incredible to me. It seemed that people would interact with me more out of duty than out of friendship and despite the condition this was obvious. There was so much shame.

The same was the case for cognitive difficulties. Concentration was too poor to read during any of the downs. Memory of anything that wasn't said in the last five minutes without extreme difficulty was impossible. Therefore, the creation of cognitive methods that put a Band-Aid on these inabilities was done with skill. For instance, it was common to get lost in the details of any narrative, written or spoken. This prompted the creation of a method of summation that was done each and every time after someone talked to me. In this method, everything read or heard was internally paraphrased in a way to make it easier to remember. For this paragraph, for instance, "description of memory problems" would be repeated internally while the person was speaking. This was effective but the flaw of it was forgetting what was said so quickly that it was rendered only mildly effective. Also, I wouldn't be able to keep up because of having to constantly paraphrase when new things were being said.

There were no tricks or workarounds that could be used for the lack of hunger that depression brings, the hardly eating that goes on and on for months, the endless lethargy, or the myriad of obsessions that depression conjures out of nothing in the unconscious of your mind. The intense obsessions that plagued every day and the horror that they bring were the involuntary catalyst of suicide.

They were particularly damaging because there was absolutely no defense against these obsessions. The best option was to try to acknowledge the obsession and to try to get involved in something else.

My many little psychological tricks for obsessions to some extent helped through the downs. But truthfully, they only really enabled faking it in order work and live in society. They were a crutch, but the leg was still broken. Medication and psychotherapy were tried at length. Living alone and living with family was tried. Focusing on meaning in general and meaning through philosophy and religion was tried. An entire assortment of vitamins and supplements were tried. But nothing worked. Nothing stopped the horror. Nothing made life bearable. Sitting over the barrel of that cold shotgun was the only comfort.

The best treatment thus far, along with work, finding meaning, and being with one of my two social pillars, was writing. There was not a single day throughout all of this that writing did not help. It is still done each and every day. It is used to document — trying to solve or at least find new pieces to the puzzle. Writing was amongst the best tools against this enormous and seemingly unbeatable giant. A daily journal was written in and each entry filled at least a couple of pages each day. The journaling served as another psychotherapist — and an excellent one at that. It validated everything to write it down.

Writing longer books, such as novels, was another tremendous strength. There is escape in the pages of a book. I wrote four books in a four-year span at that time and learned that writing is amongst the very best of ways to endure, transcend, create meaning, and fend off the mood giant I battled.

One treatment not tried, because it was so off limits to me, was the company of peers. I only had a few girlfriends through all of this because most of the year Mr. Hyde was present and I was afraid to go outside and it rendered dating impossible. What was the point even putting effort into any personal relationship? I was usually able to find female companionship when hypomanic — Dr. Jekyll — but would inevitably lose her when in the depressions — Mr. Hyde.

I found Tanya at work. She was a counselor at the halfway house. She is tall and energetic and pretty and, most of all, she is good and she changed everything.

It was Dr. Jekyll who connected with her, of course. We met at a coffee shop once. Within two months, we moved in together. She and I really bonded and fell in love fast. I asked her to move in together within a few months. I always worked fast and furiously in what little time there was to change life for the better. By the end of the manic cycle, I ended up on one knee on a beach in Maine.

However, despite the rush, it should be clearly stated that there was no dishonesty. A clearly stated and agreed to condition of the marriage was that we could not get married until she saw one full depression. After that, we could say our vows. She clung on through the down (this one was eight months) and said she was particularly scared when she saw the rage that resulted in hitting myself that was common in the self-loathing of the depressions. We got married in July of 2013.

Despite having an immensely supportive wife and mother, there was still such self-hatred toward my body throughout the depressions. Each bout brought a strong wind of wanting to destroy my carnal self and there was no concern with what happened to the physical being. As noted in the previous paragraph, I used to hit myself regularly during the downs out of sheer frustration and disdain for this malfunctioning body. This and many other delusional activities would obviously startle my wife, Tanya, and serve as an impediment to the progression of our relationship. But she has stayed and we have been together for twelve years and married for ten and a half at the time of this writing.

One facet of this new relationship with Tanya that was misperceived to be positive was having someone in — or close to — my own peer group. Tanya is seven years younger than me. Mom was thirty-six years older and Angelo is twenty-eight years older. So the relationship with Tanya was one of the only relationships with someone near my peer group and it was expected to serve as a small crutch toward socialization with peers. Unfortunately, this hypothesis was incorrect and Tanya's ability to socialize has always created more estrangement and less confidence about socializing since I cannot do it with any success. She makes friends very easily and what ended up happening was just that: she'd make friends and I wouldn't. So that desire was abandoned. Many people with bipolar disorder feel alienated from the world — and there is no exception here.

The year we met, 2012, was fifteen years since the bipolar nightmare began. Hope of a solution had faded. Outside of transcranial magnetic stimulation and electroconvulsive therapy, there seemed to be no "mainstream" treatment left untried. When it came to alternative treatments, there were even fewer left untried. There was another anticonvulsant or radical medical treatment here or there, but all of these have brought more anguish than help. What was the point? The resolutions of the medical profession always added more terror to the experience.

I walked into the familiar doors of the psychiatric clinic without any hope left to meet the new doctor at a local mental health clinic in 2013. The depression was as brutal as always. This one created such fear socially that Tanya had to sit in on the appointment in order to be able to handle going. The doctor was about forty-five minutes from where we lived and we both had to take off from work to go. My body was thirty pounds lighter and it was inhaling little and very harsh Italian cigars heavily.

The doctor was a strong willed African-American woman. She was remarkably well-versed in her craft.

"You've tried a lot," she said, looking at a fifteen page self-summary that I wrote. All psychiatrists of mine receive a copy. It summarizes everything, including the medications I took.

"I have, yes," I said nervously and defeated.

"It says here that you took Lithium," she said, analyzing the page intently. "Describe what happened on it."

"It built up in my system for about two weeks and then, with only a few warnings, I began violently vomiting — forty-four times in two days. Mom was so scared because the vomiting was so violent that I could not function. I almost had to go to the hospital. I was started at 950 mg."

"Why don't we try again?" The doctor asked sternly. She had a military background, was very educated, and had a forceful way about her. She was very kind, however, and I could see that kindness in her eyes.

"Because it's terrifying."

"Well, I'm going to titrate your dose up so slowly that I could give you a lot of reassurance that it is incredibly unlikely that you will have that reaction again," she said. "It is an extremely effective medication for bipolar disorder as severe as yours."

It seemed reasonable. And what was left to try? I consented to it and the next round of medication began. It was like participating in the real life version of *One Flew over the Cuckoo's Nest.*

The doctor was true to everything she said. She titrated the dose up in the smallest increments to get to the right dose. She was happy with the blood levels on 1200 mg. The result was the answer to my prayers. Dr. Jones saved my life by the way she prescribed Lithium and her insightfulness was invaluable that Lithium was the drug this brain needed. The gratitude was beyond comprehension.

There was no vomiting at all with the way she prescribed it. It was administered so cautiously that my body was able to metabolize it seamlessly.

The metamorphosis with Lithium was incredible. It was so surreal. To this day, eight years after Lithium, there is still the horror and constant expectation that the Faustian devil of bipolar depression will come to drag me, kicking and screaming, back into its pit. But it has not come again — miraculously it has not. Lithium was a life-saving miracle.

Are there side effects? Of course.

Are they daily? Yes.

Are they worth it? 150% worth it.

Nothing can describe the absolute horror of bipolar depression.

Lithium is effective based on blood level. That is how toxicity is measured as well. The lithium levels never get above the recommended .08 level. The level that works for this body has always been around .06 – .07 and it has always been maintained at this level. I am scared of Lithium at a toxic level, such as the toxic level reached through a doctor's poor prescribing in Pennsylvania, because at a toxic level, Lithium can be very dangerous. That is so horrifying that a blood test is gotten every three months just to check it and make certain that it is not too high.

Lithium completely eradicated Hyde from this life. It was miraculous. It transformed consciousness and enabled me to escape endlessly getting hurled to the ground by the formidable giant of bipolar depression.

In many ways, Lithium is reminiscent of Dionysius. Dionysius is the Greek god of wine. He is, in Greek mythology, a very complex figure. For instance, he was the god of ecstasy and at the same time of insanity. Lithium is also complex. It can be the most wonderful and life-saving drug, but if it gets toxic it could be the most fearful drug. It can cause goiters, damage your kidneys, and if it gets to a toxic level in my body, it could wreak utter destruction.

For almost fifteen years, there were a variety of methods learned and utilized to endure bipolar disorder. The term endure is used because I was not beating it. It was worked around. Reading. Studying. Psychotherapy. Being with loved ones. Changing surroundings. All was tried but nothing worked to beat this giant.

Then, Lithium was found — thanks to Dr. Jones. It has enabled my brain to live as if I don't even have the debilitating disorder. This Kafka-esque existence changed into a comparatively peaceful one. It chemically eradicated almost every symptom of depression and mania – all at once.

It is important to note that Lithium was needed to overcome my bipolar disorder. There are few maladies in the human condition that one can defeat alone. We can be made stronger by all maladies but few can be completely overcome individualistically. We all need help. This is an immutable truth. However, the heavy hand of our individualistic culture often blinds us to this truth and can eventually break our will to keep getting up and getting stronger.

Furthermore, if there is any one character trait that helped overcome bipolar disorder, it is humility. Endurance and belief that life is suffering helps too, but humility is what enabled asking for help and realize that the world is not going to stop because I have a problem.

Humility may be the best of things. Humility is the enemy of arrogance and arrogance destroys people. There is little hope for an arrogant person with infirmities but possibilities are endless for the meek and for the humble who have the same conditions.

Even my humility cannot be claimed as my own. It was given to me by the Bible — by Christ — who, to me, exemplified humility for us. I took His teachings and tried to apply to them to all facets of my life — very imperfectly. It was humility that enabled me to admit a problem existed, to embrace alienation and a terrible identity, to concede the need for others, to agree to treatments, and so on and so forth.

I cannot emphasize enough the importance of humility in beating your giants.

I would especially need this humility at age eighteen. This was the age at which the traumatic brain was suffered. It would throw me to the ground in an entirely new and terrifying way.

II

TRAUMATIC BRAIN INJURY

ON FEBRUARY 10, 2001, Dad woke up early as was his custom even on Saturdays. He awoke to find that I was not in bed. I was eighteen-years-old and in my second semester at college. I was eighteen years old and in my second semester of college (a "young scholars" program allowed me to take college credits in high school). I lived at home with Mom and Dad and went to the local satellite campus of Penn State.

Friday night was party night. That was not peculiar to Dad. However, I always returned in the early morning hours on Saturday. Dad found it upsetting that I was not lying peacefully in my twin bed. He was worried and is the type of person who always believes the worst possible scenario. Last time I didn't come home, he said that he was ready to start going to all the local lakes, ponds, and streams to look for the dead body.

The parties were always with the same group of people.

They were the group with whom my time was spent in high school and some were from grade school. We were almost all very familiar with each other. It should be no surprise, then, that I was comfortable getting inebriated with them. In fact, they introduced me to both alcohol and drugs.

I resisted substances until tenth grade. Tenth grade was age fifteen. This was when the cycles of bipolar disorder really began. Once they hit, it was too much to handle. I just couldn't take it. I began to be a very zealous fan of The Doors, was driven by gaining psychological relief, and began asking, *Why resist drugs and alcohol when they seem to offer an escape? Why do everything right when there is no relief from it?*

I'll never forget the first drink I ever had. It was in the woods next to a nearby lake. It was whiskey. It was winter. The alcohol eliminated the shivering very quickly. The two people who invited me to join them were also the ones who bought the alcohol, were drunk themselves, and encouraged the drinking. It was in that moment that I remember looking at the dark night sky and a large bright moon. Life seemed much better with alcohol in me — the doldrums of depression faded.

Alcohol seemed as good a treatment option as any. I drank daily after that and always came home.

On February 10, 2001, I didn't come home. I have tried to imagine that morning from Mom and Dad's point of view many times. Mom always slept a little later. Dad got up at the crack of dawn each day for his job and was always up early on the weekends.

There sat Dad, alone, when the sun was just beginning to show itself behind the clouds of the winter sky. In our house, it was intensely quiet in the mornings. The only sound is that of the clocks: tick, tock, tick, tock, tick, tock. After breakfast, when the car wasn't in the driveway, some panic must have set in.

Mom found it alarming as well. After they collaborated, they first called a young man, Mark, who lived a few doors down in our development. He came to the area in fourth grade and I befriended him and we were close ever since.

"Do you know where Kurt is?" Dad asked. "He didn't come home last night."

"Uhh, no, haven't seen him," he lied.

I was often with Mark. So this made Mom and Dad panic more. They made some other calls to people who composed my social network. They got similar answers. By this time, they were truly upset. They called Mark back. They asked again,

"Where is our son?" This time they got a response that was at least mildly accurate.

"I believe he still at Kieran's. We were there last night. That was the last I saw him."

My Dad called Kieran's mother immediately.

"Kurt was at your house last night. He did not come home. We are wondering where he is?"

"He's fine. I'm just feeding him spaghetti in order to sober him up," she lied.

About an hour passed. Mom and Dad were less panicked now that they were assured that everything was okay.

They didn't know it, but every second that Kieran's mother delayed my parent's coming to get me, blood was pumping onto my brain from a broken artery. I lay unconscious. I was dying.

I was lying there with this blood pumping all over my skull from around 1 AM when the left vertebral artery in my brain was broken by so-called friends, until nine in the morning, when his mother called back.

She called and simply said, "You better come pick up your son." For something like eight hours, I laid on a piece of cardboard in her basement. There was vomit everywhere and the smell of vomit was all over. My clothes were wet from water that everybody splashed throughout the night to wake me up.

When Dad came, they had me propped up in a chair. He had to walk down the steps into a dark and smoky basement. The basement was so dark that it was hard for him to see. They wanted it that way. He remembered that I was in a chair, a recliner. He said that my head was tilted back and eyes were rolled back. My right leg was all that showed life. It was pointed straight out and shook very actively.

This is what occurred that night. On February 9, I went to the normal Friday night escape and drowned myself in alcohol with people who were perceived as friends and believed could be trusted. There was a girl there and we went to my car to have some privacy sometime after midnight. We wanted more privacy, away from where there were lights showing. The car was backed up and it bumped into Kieran's brother's car. The next thing I heard was a loud pounding on the car window. A dark figure forcefully demanded the keys from me.

It gets very hazy after that. I likely underwent a sort of Kafkaesque trial for nicking his brothers car. What I do know is that in the end, I endured what my neurosurgeon wrote in his notes was a "strangulation type injury/neck twist." The force of this broke my left vertebral artery, one of the major arteries that feed the brain.

They then dragged my lifeless body onto a piece of cardboard in the basement. I laid there on that cardboard all night. The blood from that broken artery continually gushed all over my brain. The doctors called it a forced stroke. Every minute that passed — every hour that care was delayed — greatly decreased any chance at survival and, more importantly, greatly diminished the chance of a decent quality of life.

Where were all the people I went to school with all my life, hung out with every day, and, in one case, called family? They went home. Each and every one of them went home. It was like a scene from *High Noon.* There was Kurt lying on a mat, seizing violently and completely unresponsive. All these so-called friends went home and one even lied to Mom and Dad when they called and asked about it.

This was the first time that environmental factors —

horrible people — and not biological factors — mental problems — threw me to the ground. The epiphany I had was while the cause may have been different, the mechanisms to get back up were the same.

After Dad called the ambulance, my dying body was taken to the hospital and put in intensive care. I was there for forty days. It was here where my life was saved.

Dr. Sedor was the best neurosurgeon in the area. He was called in that Saturday due to the emergency. He came in and acted immediately.

Before he operated, the Last Rites were administered. The Last Rites are given by Catholic priests and are given to people who are about to die. That's how expected it was that I would not be alive.

Dr. Sedor had many decisions to make. Above all, he had to choose how to operate as he had to operate immediately.

As it was explained, he had two broad choices: either he could give the best chance at very uncertain life, but it would be certain that my quality of life would be greatly diminished (vegetative state, wheelchair); or he could operate in such a way that gave the best chance of a quality life, but made it extremely unlikely that I'd live.

The latter at least gave the possibility of having a life that wasn't wrought with even more torture, so he chose that, with Mom and Dad's consent. He opened my skull and let the blood out. He cut out much of left side of the cerebellum, which was dead from the stroke and from all the time that had passed. According to the National Library of Medicine, the entire cerebellum contains around eighty percent of all of the neurons in the entire brain. Losing half was a tremendous loss. He then put a clip on the left vertebral artery to stop the bleeding onto the brain.

This saved my life. But nobody knew what to expect in terms of how functional this new Kurt would be. Mom and Dad were told that while I was alive, it was extremely likely that there would be a different person emerging — if any person emerged at all. I was in the most severe coma that someone could be in.

Mom always said that she never forgot the moment that consciousness returned. There were tubes coming out of almost everywhere — tubes were in my head, down the throat, attached to the chest, in the nose, and so on. I motioned to Mom for a pen and paper since speaking was impossible. She gave them. I wrote, "eye secretions" on the pad. Both Mom and Dad gasped in relief. If I could write eye secretions, the cognition was clearly intact. This is what they believed and it was immensely relieving.

I obviously cannot remember much of this. However, when it was being experienced, others stated I was acutely aware of everything that was going on. For instance, both hands were tied to the bed for about nine days. This was done so that I would not continue to rip the tubes out my nose, mouth, and throat. There were so many tubes.

Being tied to the bed was infuriating and caused significant psychological damage. I can distinctly remember the rage. The visitation of hate was on an entirely new level. It was like the embodiment of pure anger. Everything agitated and anger formed itself into a metaphorical tidal wave of rage. Fierce anger was constant. It was illogical at times but it was very real nonetheless.

I had a stroke of the cerebellum. It was a forced stroke caused by the severe trauma. The left vertebral artery was broken by the assault. Because they let this artery bleed onto my brain all night and didn't get help, the bleeding clogged all of the brain's meninges. This made it so that the cerebral spinal fluid was not able to escape. In other words, the fluid that is in the skull just accumulated in the skull. This created more and more pressure, like a balloon getting filled with water. This caused tremendous distress. The pressure caused by this fluid caused double-vision.

The condition of too much cerebrospinal fluid on the cranium is called *hydrocephalus*. To relieve it, a shunt needed to be installed. This was another surgery, about two months after the original injury. The ventriculoperitoneal shunt installation meant my skull had to be opened a second time. The shunt has a mechanism that allows the fluid in when too much cerebrospinal fluid fills up my head. The shunt drains through a tube that was fished through the neck and down the chest and into the stomach.

Then there was the *vasospasm.* A vasospasm is a severe constriction of the arteries in the brain. It can cause any number of issues, including tissue death. Therefore, the body underwent another nightmare and was thrown to the ground yet again. The result of the vasospasm was even more brain damage in a number of areas.

Most of this is beyond recollection. But there is plenty stored in my consciousness. Memory is strongly affected by emotions. That is why rage is so easily recalled. I also remember being woken up from blessed sleep endlessly through the nights, partly because it created fury. The nurses would come every hour or so — there was no sense of time — and they would grab my hands or toes and would make me grab their hands. They would say something that affirmed consciousness like, "Can you feel squeezing?" And only then can I return to blessed sleep. Sleeping was something that had to be done sitting up now.

There was this guy named "Frankie" in one of the hospitals. Frankie had a heavy accent. He screamed, "I no want! I no want!" for what seemed like hours. He kept complaining in such a loud Italian voice that ensured there would not be any slipping into unconsciousness. And sleep was necessary to avoid the Dante's Inferno that now pervaded an already odious existence.

The only positive memory was Mom. She was an Italian woman and beautiful and I can remember the light of the moon shining onto her face from the hospital window at night. She had taut skin that forms slight indentations around her jaw. She slept many nights in the hospital on two chairs that faced each other. She would sit in one chair and her legs rested out on the other. She reclined the best she could. They were kitchen chairs so it was obviously intensely uncomfortable. I was forced to wake up so often at night and only remember being so grateful that she was there. She was the reason that shouldering on was possible. That is, she was the reason that anger did not win.

After the brain injury, it was like becoming an infant again: everything had to be relearned. So we became extremely emotionally close and our bonds were strong and seeing her devotedly and self-sacrificingly laying there was very powerful.

I can also remember the dizziness. If you've ever spun around in a circle over and over to the point wherein you fall, it was similar to that. However, it didn't relent. The dizziness was all encompassing. It made walking confused and disoriented and impossible. This was expected by the doctors. Dad always pushed around my wheelchair. As he did, I would hear him say, "Zoom zoom zoom!" mimicking a ridiculous car commercial slogan at the time. For some reason this was endlessly hilarious.

In the final analysis, I could not walk. I could not talk. I had a paralyzed vocal cord due to what was done to me and the brain damage all over. My voice sounded, at best, like Don Corleone in *The Godfather*, and at worst, a whisper. There was a wealth of new psychological scars from the false friends, each of whom turned their backs when help was needed most and would make any trust of anyone almost impossible from that point forward.

The doctor who saved me, and all of his staff, referred to me as "Miracle Man." Dr. Sedor was like an angel and either him or one of his assistants were always near and ready to answer any question and be of any assistance.

"You're lucky to be here," a nurse would say. "We're calling you 'miracle man' because you had virtually no chance of survival, let alone surviving in a higher functioning state."

I just nodded. Nothing about consciousness felt very lucky as I looked at a seemingly endless network of tubes running out of my body.

"You must be here for a reason," another nurse would chime in. "I don't know if you are spiritual but your survival in the fully functional state you're in was said to be next to impossible," she said with a kind grin. "You have a calling — a purpose — to be on this earth," she went on and my eyes scanned her and saw a crucifix fastened around her neck. They were encouraging and there was great appreciation for what they told me.

Dr. Sedor explained that I had almost no shot of living and even less of a shot of functioning cognitively or physically. Just moving around was a "blessing" now.

I saw the situation very differently. It was simply a new nightmare that had to be confronted. There was a day many months after the hospital when I was sitting in a lawn chair in the backyard of my family's house after all the surgeries from the head injury. I was looking at the sky and was feeling the warm summer air drift across my skin. I looked upward toward the sky and asked, "Is that enough torture now? Whatever was done wrong was paid for, right? It's all going to be good from now on, right?"

There was no answer. But the suffering had just begun. Somehow with these horrific experiences, the worst was still yet to come.

It seemed there was no way to be made stronger by this nightmare. But that is the task and that is the reason for this book. That is the role of Antaeus.

There is deep gratitude to a great many people for my recovery from severe traumatic brain injury. It was said that I would never walk. But now I do walk — and walk extremely well — and am very grateful for it.

I spent about a year in an inpatient and then intensive outpatient rehabilitation facility. There were those big bouncing balls. There were endless amounts of hands under my armpits and arms trying to make sure I stay balanced and did not fall again. I remember hearing instruction after instruction stating to do the most inane and absurd movements over and over and over again.

There were many problems due to the traumatic brain injury. The most pressing, after the hospital and rehab, was equilibrium. The cerebellum governs equilibrium — balance. There was no balance. Falling down was constant. I could stand straight up but just fell like a cut tree within a minute. Dad always stated that in the neurosurgeon's office, I would just fall down if someone wasn't holding on to me. I was spinning in dizziness when sitting down as well. It was all day and all night. And I needed — and am grateful for — the people who helped every bit of the way.

The physical therapists gave all manner of exercises to do. The speech therapist gave all sorts of talking exercises to get the vocal cord to come back. The cognitive therapist worked on memory and rage. Mom and Dad took me to see them most of the days of the week. Every moment of it was horrible. But it was necessary and helped immensely.

Then, there were Mom and Dad and their tireless efforts to get me well from the terror of my condition. When the winter receded and spring was brought to northeastern Pennsylvania, they would walk me around the yard every day. They were tireless in terms of helping execute all of the exercises that were given to get better. They would do anything and everything to bring me back. They were the greatest environmental assets against the slings and arrows of the head injury.

My favorite physical activities were always sports. I played baseball, for instance, for fourteen years of my life. So, Dad bought one of those plastic bats for small children, the ones with the enormous barrel so that a toddler could make contact.

Mom exclaimed in her loving tone,"Go hit the ball, honey!"

And my Dad followed her with, "Let's give it a shot."

As I gradually became able to stand for longer periods of time, we used them. Dad pitched soft, easy pitches in our woodsy backyard. Our German Shepherd was always ready to collect the balls and watched eagerly and excitedly. We used to engage in this activity constantly before the injury and so we began trying after it.

I am a good contact hitter and seldom strike out. But despite the fact that the ball was so big and the bat was so big, I could not hit it no matter what. Over and over and over the bat missed the ball. There was not a single time the bat connected with that ball. It was incredible to watch this body utterly incapable of doing something that it had done forever. It was truly being knocked to the ground and having to get back up over and over again. The head injury taught the concept of failing but forging ahead.

Activities such as these helped lot. After very literally getting knocked down and getting back up over and over and over again, this body miraculously found a way to walk. This means the rest of my cerebellum was miraculously able to take over the responsibilities for the part that was lost.

Today, when seeing a neurosurgeon, the same test is administered every time. The tests involve touching my nose with both index fingers and walking a straight line and doing other things that measure dexterity and balance. Then the conversation almost always goes like this:

"That's incredible," the neurosurgeon says.

"What is, doctor?"

"Well, I can see you don't have a left side of your cerebellum. There is no difference between the way you move and the way anyone who has both sides of the cerebellum moves."

The recovery of my cerebellum, of course, was achieved through the remarkable healing powers of the body. It was also achieved with the help of others and especially through hard and tireless work. I failed and fell innumerable times. Those falls did not feel like they were making me stronger emotionally, but strength was definitely growing biologically. The wonderful cerebellum used the negative impact of falling and getting back up to help fix itself and found ways to compensate.

Falling down quite literally made me stronger and I am very grateful for it.

After about a year, it was common for the neighbors to see a young brain injured man running out for passes with Mom as the quarterback. She had quite an arm and there was never more gratitude to catch a football. That gratitude is always felt. And I have caught thousands of footballs since the injury. Tanya throws them now.

The paralyzed vocal cord came back, too. Speech therapy was okay, but what really helped my vocal cord return was singing. I sang constantly. On the way to the therapist, singing. On the way back, singing. Through the week, singing. My voice, at best, was like a very, very soft and bad version of Louis Armstrong's voice. It was a soft and throaty sound. I am grateful that Mom and Dad could stand it.

Little by little, the vocal cord grew stronger. My favorite band is The Doors. Jim Morrison, the lead singer, has a very deep voice. Every attempt was made to mimic it. And eventually, it was possible. The vocal cord came back. It was slow but it was sure. After a time, four months or so, the voice returned and sounded as it did before the injury. It was wonderful. And like walking, there was an entirely new gratitude for having a voice that remains to this day.

My body was able to walk after it was, literally, bedridden. My vocal cord was able to work again after it was paralyzed. The doctor never thought it was possible.

How was it like Antaeus, though?

Psychologically, as with any malady, I became Antaeus. As Antaeus, there was a conscious effort to survey the environment for strengths — for things in the environment that could help work around or soothe the problem. There was no autonomy as everything required someone's help. Mom, Dad, or a nurse was needed to do anything outside of the bed. Furthermore, getting one of them to come was a challenge because no one could hear the feckless and whispering voice that came out.

The most poignant lesson was learning how fragile and helpless we essentially are. I learned how horrifying this helplessness is. Perhaps worst of all was realizing that this fragility and helplessness does not make it better.

Enter the philosophy and psychotherapeutic approach of existentialism. Just being helpless was not an end in itself. Even though it was not my fault, the traumatic brain injury was mine, and therefore I had to take responsibility for it. I had to take responsibility for the raw deal that was given and had to do something with it. This is a tenant of existentialism, which focuses, in part, on the concept of our responsibility.

How could this be achieved? Enter Antaeus.

By taking responsibility, no one is saying to go at it alone or without help. No one can do that. Others are needed. I would never have learned to walk, to talk, or to manage life in any way without Mom and Dad. Mom spent every waking moment with me until autonomy could be achieved.

The point here is this: *everyone is responsible for dealing with their lot in life no matter how undeserved or unjust it is.*

We all need assistance, however, of all kinds to improve ourselves. No one can overcome all the problems on their own. The formula was simple: *Lower pride. Embrace humility. Accept help.*

The tireless motive is always getting better. This was a centerpiece of strategy in all of my maladies.

There were countless other lessons. For instance, all the brain research cumulated in an excellent understanding of the brain. This showed how incredibly resourceful and resilient the human body is. It was a major goal to replicate this resiliency from a psychological standpoint. The body found a way around every insult to it to function normally. It was my task to do the same to what ails the brain psychologically and physiologically.

Memory is one such insult that would not get better on its own. Memory was and continues to be an ongoing battle.

"Did you like the show we watched last Tuesday?" Tanya asked me.

"I don't remember watching a show. What show?"

About a thousand versions of this conversation occur each day for me. I forget everything. This was originally written twenty years after my head injury. If you put any time between this bruised and battered brain and the event, person, or place, there is still a lot of trouble remembering it. It just fades into darkness.

Right after the head injury, it was said that I could not recall what occurred a few minutes ago. Someone would walk into a room with me, talk, and then leave. Upon their return, even if it was five minutes later, I had to be prompted as to what we spoke about.

It borders on humor to say that I cannot remember how long this went on. Needless to say, it was immensely frustrating. A few emotionally based memories did slip through into my long term memory.

The only option was to accept responsibility for my new memory and find ways to work around it.

Writing everything down was the first step. After the injury, I kept a little pocket notebook in which I wrote many, many things that I could not depend on my memory to recall. In no time, the act of writing down everything began improving memory drastically. The notebook and constant repetition of using it enabled great progress to be made.

"Do you remember what day it is, honey?" Mom would ask kindly. There was never a time when the answer was produced correctly. The new memory had a peculiar facet to it. It could recall much of what occurred during the current day — only for that day. Sleep was like using an eraser on the chalkboard of memory. After sleeping, all was forgotten.

So, notes became the primary technique. "You are reading *The Stranger* with Mom today." This was written on a piece of notebook paper along with several other activities for the day. This prompted memory and more often than not, it worked. This was the method used to limp along doing this each day every day for around five years.

It was very arduous. This system of handwritten notes required a constant supply of paper that was readily accessible, a pen, and immense organization. There were — and are today — so many scraps of paper all around with little notes on them. They can get extremely confusing. But, by and large, this method works.

This note system has been used for twenty years now. It has gotten me through undergraduate and graduate school. During classes, in all of the books, summaries of what the author meant were written in the margins. I developed all kinds of techniques and methods to remember things. They do not work all the time, but by and large they work. Many, many books were read on memory and mnemonic devices and many other memory aids were utilized. The memory after the brain injury is poor. But it is functional. The conversations several doctors had regarding memory sounded something like this,

"After five years, your memory will stop improving," a neurosurgeon told me. "After the fifth year, you can consider that your baseline memory."

This sent terror down my spine. It was as if I was in a race.

"But there's no set number of years, right doctor? It could be six or seven years for me, right?"

The doctor could always see the effort to conjure some hope. "It could. But, unfortunately, it is generally five years," he said firmly.

It has been twenty three years and this battered memory is still improving. It, like the rest of the brain, is remarkably resilient. You may not know it, but you have this resilience, too.

None of this improvement is ever seamless. At least once per day, it becomes clear that the statement being made has already been said. Facial cues have been remarkably effective at revealing who has already heard the information being conveyed. One skill that has been polished is one similar to Sherlock Holmes, surveying the faces of others — and especially their eyes — to survey the repetitiveness of comments and questions due to the lack of memory. It works, too. It is very helpful. I remark, "I've already told you this, haven't I?"

They nod.

"Have I told you about my condition?"

Whoever the person is, we generally both laugh. That question is a reference to the movie *Memento*, a film in which the protagonist has a memory condition that does not allow him to remember things for more than a few seconds.

Humor remains an extremely effective way to deal with adversity. It can, to a small extent replace some of the rage and frustration. Memory issues will be a lifelong difficulty. However, through elaborate note methods, humor, and humility, it has been very manageable. Almost no one knows of these memory problems unless they are told at this point.

Another deficit from the head injury has been issues with anger. The rage felt when it occurred was legendary fury. It was the rage of Achilles. It was a rage with the strength of a tidal wave behind it. It made my face red and the hair would actually stand up on my arms. I almost literally saw red. The trembling was fierce. The anger brought with it a headache that is so powerful it was as if my head would explode. The anger actually seemed tangible it was so real. It was so strong that it was like being under the influence of a drug.

It is important to note that this rage of Achilles was not acted on — most of the time. Every once in a while all that anger would come flooding out. However, learning control of it was — and is — vital.

Understanding how to control anger is a monumental task. It is not something that comes quickly, either.

In George Orwell's book *1984,* he depicts a society controlled by a totalitarian government. In an effort for the government to deflect anger away from itself, it implements "the two minutes hate." The government films the enemies of society and forces the citizens to watch the film. During the two minutes hate, the citizens are allowed to yell and express all of their hatred at the enemies of the state for a full two minutes.

Similarly, after the head injury, there was an Orwellian "hour hate" developed for each day. For an hour each day, I sat in a rocking chair and allowed the hate and anger at everything that happened pour out. Regular smoking started after the head injury, which is very common. However, the smoking occurred too much. This was probably a sort of unconscious yearning for death. It felt very good at the time and I smoked during the one hour hate eagerly each day.

However, it was useless. Thinking about the party and how much irritation it brought may have felt good in the short term. But it was useless. Worse than useless, the argument can be made that it was actually hurting. This rationalization ended the one hour hates. It was not a therapeutic way to process feelings. A decision was made to control the rage rather than indulge it. Indulging it was not working.

Controlling the rage seemed to be an entirely reachable goal due to my reasoning capacity. I could not and cannot help feeling furious, but could also reason through it so that there was never a thought to act on it or cultivate it. To give an example, the self-talk of the rage sounded like this:

> *This horrible thing was done to me and the world is so unjust. They will never know the pain they've caused mentally or physically and it is completely unfair.*

Then there was a pivot to reasoning through the feeling:

> *It was a despicable thing that they did and a remarkable betrayal. However, your hatred and anger cannot do a single thing about it. Anger will not get you your cerebellum back or take away all the suffering you or your parents have gone through. They did it and it is done. Dwelling on your anger only continues to let them hurt you. No matter how hard it is, wish them well and let it go. There is so much work to do to get better.*

It was through thousands of versions of this self-talk that control was gained over anger. It was and is very hard and it takes many attempts and hard work. However, one universal rule of overcoming adversity is doing hard work. Getting up off the ground after being thrown down so many times is incredibly hard work.

The head injury was the latest in series of nightmares that brought this existence to the brink of suicide many times over many years. It, like the bipolar disorder, was and is horrific. I still carry all the scars – psychological and physical – from it. It will, like bipolar disorder, always be present and its wounds will always create fear. The trust issues developed from the incredible betrayal were immense. The trust issues impede consciousness each and every day.

Trusting anyone remains difficult. However, it, like bipolar, made me stronger. Help was needed to stand up again. There was the need for biological help, help from doctors, help changing thought patterns, help with faith and especially help from Mom and Dad. All of that taught more lessons about humility. The TBI had the effect of giving me a degree in how powerless I actually am in this world and that powerlessness created an immense amount of humility. It became clear that it takes falling down a thousand times — sometimes literally — to be able to get up and stay up. The lessons were in perseverance and strength and hate and rage and love and forgiveness all at the same time.

The other lesson was in regard to the incredibly complex brain. The more reading that is done, the more one realizes how little one knows about that remarkably complex organ. Hundreds of tricks were created to remember things and many were self-created. These and many more lessons are why I am stronger for having suffered a very severe brain injury. These and many more reasons are why the head injury made me become like Antaeus.

III

OBSESSIVE COMPULSIVE DISORDER

OBSESSIVE COMPULSIVE DISORDER WAS chronologically the first giant that opened the doors into the struggle that is this existence. It is also my earliest memory on this earth. I remember, at five years old, looking at each footstep and counting. It was at Epcot Center, Orlando, Florida. I was walking next to Mom and Dad in a place that is, to a kid, supposed to be the greatest place on earth.

Despite the fact that images of Mickey Mouse surrounded me and that rides, games, and fun were in every direction, my inner world was in turmoil. I was counting each and every footstep. "1-2-3-4-5-6-7-8," was said very softly with each step. The footsteps had to end in an even number or something bad would happen to Mom and Dad. That was everything. That's all that mattered.

It didn't stop once we left Florida. The counting obsession lasted many years. And it wasn't just with footsteps. Hours per day were spent catching the football, hitting the baseball, shooting the basketball, or kicking the soccer ball looking to count to the "correct number" of catches, hits, shots, or kicks. The toothbrush had to be used with the correct number of strokes — a specific number on each tooth — or any number of tragedies would befall Mom or Dad or me. There really wasn't anything that evaded counting – even the number of times a word was used in discourse with someone. Books even had to be stopped on even pages. This was OCD's first manifestation — first obsession — and it dominated the youngest years of this existence.

The obsessions were counted because everything was counted. In a single day, there are between five hundred to over one thousand compulsions from OCD. This was as true at a young age as it is today. The endless daily flood of obsessions is powerful and incredibly numerous.

Obsessive compulsive disorder (OCD) is like an evil puppeteer. Fear is its primary tool. Fear is what composes the metaphorical strings that it uses to animate its puppet. The fear is created by the obsessions and the obsessions inevitably cause deep terror and vulnerability. OCD exploits this vulnerability through compulsions and they are obeyed because of the fear of the obsessions. In this way, it seeks full control over its puppet — and often gets it. There are an endless amount of movements/obsessions and its puppets, like me, can end up spending one hundred percent of their day being controlled by it. To this day, and even writing this now, from morning until night, command after command, order after order is demanded. The puppeteer lords over everything in life and tries to make itself a god.

But I won't allow it. I used religion to make obedience to OCD equivalent to worshipping a false idol. Education, psychotherapy, medication, and other weapons are used to battle this giant. It has thrown me to the ground every day since at least five years old and continues to do so each and every day. However, it is manageable. Only people who know me very well can see it is there. Others cannot see it unless they are told or unless they monitor me very closely. Every day when OCD's commands throw me to the ground, because there are so many other obsessions than counting, a way has been found to get up stronger and beat it back with my knowledge and other tools.

The counting was dominant for years. However, then it just minimized or phased into the background as the next major obsession rolled in to plague life. OCD runs on these obsessions and every obsession is attached to a compulsion that is designed to assuage the anxiety of the obsession. Therefore, all day, every day, I am tossed to the ground by obsession after obsession and believe my compulsions will somehow be protection from the anxiety of the obsession.

The next OCD stage consisted of doubting as the obsession, checking as the compulsion. Counting was still there, but checking became dominant. Doubting, which is the obsession that led to checking, continues to be a large part of existence today. There were always struggles to leave Mom's house or my house or even office for fear of a fire starting.

"I cooked eggs this morning. I am sure the stove was left on."

I checked. The stove is off. All four knobs are stared at and all the burners are touched. It is clear it is off. Before I can get into the car to leave the doubting thought comes like thunder, "The stove is on. One of the burners was slightly turned — and it is actually on."

So I go back. Off. The process repeats within five minutes. If feelings were the boss, I wouldn't ever leave my own house today or Mom's house when I was younger. This obsession simply consumes me.

This is the general mechanism of the doubting obsession and checking compulsion. OCD finds just about everything can be checked. Everything is checked — all day, every day. Whatever is cared about must be checked so that it hasn't changed or vanished or gone away. If I am late for anything, it is due to checking. If it is not checked, something terrible will happen to whatever is most dear. Everything must be checked — or else.

Doubting/checking, like counting, also has to "feel" right. Not only does everything have to be ordered very specifically on the desk and everywhere else, and checked often to make sure it is perfect, it also has to feel right, or there is no leaving. I "have" to keep coming back over and over and over to check it and touch it until it is right. Doubting causes insomnia. It keeps me constantly moving.

It plagues consciousness because, as always with OCD, if not, something terrible will happen.

It is important to note that during these first two phases of OCD, being so young, I was far from being Antaeus yet. Rather, I was a helpless puppet obeying the strings of that puppeteer and not cognizant that everyone does not have to live by the same nightmarish myriad of rules.

The third phase of OCD involved an obsession with hoarding and a compulsion with saving. OCD began to attach certain feelings and qualities to inanimate objects. They felt like they were a part of me, and if given away, it was as if parts myself were given away with them. Mom, who is tremendously clean and orderly, intensely disliked the hoarding at a young age.

"Honey, you have to clean out your old clothes to make room for your new clothes. Some of the stuff has to go. You can't keep everything!" Mom pleaded.

"But there's nothing that I want to get rid of. How can I get rid of, say, this awesome sweatshirt?"

"You are going to end up just like your uncle," Mom always grumbled at the end of our hoarding conversations. My uncle was a wealthy man who was unable to separate from his money. He hoarded almost all of it. He came from the same genetic line that has OCD in the family and it is very likely that the OCD came though these genes which are prevalent in my family's genes.

The truth is that the feeling OCD gave is this: If that sweatshirt was gotten rid of, there would be the massive loss of ability to do the things once done in that sweatshirt. In other words, if I did well on a test while that sweatshirt was owned or while wearing that sweatshirt, then the only way to do well on future tests was by continuing to own and wear that sweatshirt. I did not think that as much as felt it. A great despair would possess me and I would be terrified about losing whatever abilities I was able to display while having that sweatshirt. This became particularly difficult when it came to sports. There was immense anxiety and inability to get rid of any jersey, any underwear, any bat, ball, whatever, in which a good game was played.

Along with hoarding obsessions, obsessions based on contamination and compulsions based on washing were prominent early on and remain strong today. Contamination means exaggerated fears that some perceived "contaminant" is evading my world. Getting sick was horror at a young age. So, in church, my hands were furiously rubbed down my pant legs after shaking hands with fellow parishioners, so much so they would get red and a 'burn' was felt from the friction. This was an attempt to "burn off the diseases" from their hands that they got onto my hands during the handshake. Nothing could be touched except for the fork and the knife after I washed my hands before eating. If anything else had to be touched, even the chair (which was pulled out with my leg to sit down), I had to rewash before eating.

As noted, contamination/washing, like many of the other obsessions and compulsions, are still very dominant

OCD manifestations in my life at present. The pandemic exacerbated this tenfold. My hands are washed constantly each day and at any given time have cracks in them. They bleed often from the dryness caused by the over washing. And there are many other things that are contaminated. While the contaminations vary, the "rules" for how to avoid being contaminated are all pretty similar. Contamination, in OCD land, is transmitted by association, often touch. So this is the basic thought process and feeling since the pandemic:

"There is a room with people and those people could have COVID. Their saliva particles are in that room because they are talking and breathing in the room and the shirt on me is also in the room and therefore to be safe the shirt must be washed. There are zero bases for that in science and it is an utter fantasy. But that is how OCD grows."

"Why do you have so much hand sanitizer?" is one of many questions often asked due to this obsession.

"Just being clean," I state matter-of-factly, as if everyone should use hand sanitizer thirty to forty times per day in addition to washing their hands nonstop. Hand sanitizer serves as an anti-contaminant when the "real stuff" — soap and water — isn't available.

There were — and are — so many other obsessions. For example, everything has to be symmetrical — *everything*. The external worlds that there is a sense of agency in, whether it is the rooms I inhabit, the articles on any desk, the walls around me, or in the articles of clothing in any closet must have some semblance of symmetry to "feel" right. One personal favorite manifests itself as the plaguing desire, the unstoppable itch that occurs to get reassurance when you don't feel like you're in complete control. Then there's the constant compulsion to tell every authority (boss, spouse, police, parent — it does not matter) everything that you did that was even mildly wrong or mistaken. That's a real compulsion and it creates honesty, yes, but can also take quite a toll on your life when you can never shut up about whatever you did less-than-perfectly. It's the Tell-Tale Heart manifestation of OCD and it is brutal in its own right.

Each obsession is accompanied by a compulsion each affects me greatly and takes up a great deal of time. These are just a few phases in OCD's early development. However, let it suffice to say that I was — and am — in an OCD straitjacket.

It was around eighteen years old that a revelation came. It wasn't that no one else talked about the obsessions and compulsions, it was that they didn't have obsessions and compulsions to the same extent. Some people had idiosyncrasies and were very eccentric, but these quirks were not the all-encompassing puppeteer that ruled my life. They were and are not the same.

It must be reiterated that the phases of OCD listed here are just several of the endless examples of this giant throwing me to the ground in every moment. If truth is told, there is no facet of life that OCD does not try to control. Like a spider, it spawns a web of paralyzation in the form of commands and obsessions. It tethered life to a virtual web of orders, feelings, and ideas. It often reaches the point of madness wherein OCD's web of commands is stronger than the commands and dictates of reality, itself. In other words, it completely takes over your existence. Evading OCD's punishments became a full-time vocation.

Then the change began to occur. At family gatherings, something happened. My aunt used to wear plastic latex gloves wherever she went and will not let anyone into her apartment or car. My Nonno (Italian grandfather) brushed his teeth right off his gums from obsessing on brushing each tooth perfectly each night. My uncle hoarded in spectacular fashion.

It became clear to me that there was a giant tormentor acting as a puppeteer of all my thoughts and actions. This puppeteer would not be allowed to destroy me. It would throw me to the ground, but I would get up and find a way to fight.

War with OCD began with self-disclosure. If a partner could be recruited against this menace, there was a better chance of beating it. The first person who was told about it came roughly twelve years after the beginning of the grappling with the giant on a daily basis (age five). It should come as no surprise to the reader at this point in my narrative that I told the number one support network: Mom. All of life was spent hiding the rituals from everyone. One of the giant's "rules," prior to my seventeenth year on this earth, was to hide its existence from everyone: even Mom. I did and learned to make a false excuses for everything done for OCD that people noticed and said something about. So, not even she knew throughout my life prior to seventeen. She knew I was eccentric. But she didn't know about OCD because when she was growing up, OCD was not known very well.

"Mom, I can't take it anymore," I said one day in the living room. The smell of her apple zeppoles, an Italian dessert, cooking filled the air around. "All of life is spent doing crazy things that I don't want to do. However, if I don't do it, there is something inside that makes me feel like something is going to happen to you or to Dad. I don't know what it is and don't know what to do. But even as this is being said, certain words have to be used so many times in the sentence and sentences have to be ended with certain words and everything must be ordered perfectly all the time and it's very frightening and absolutely constant." There were tears in my eyes.

Mom was incredibly supportive. She provided emotional support and did not doubt anything that was said. Almost everyone else has some variation of this reaction when telling them about the OCD rituals:

"Oh, yeah, I do a lot of things like that, too. I have to lick the bottom of the spoon before I can eat my ice cream on top of the spoon. It's ridiculous! But I know exactly what you're talking about. You're not sick! It's normal!"

These reactions serve to trivialize a very serious problem and are incredibly irritating.

But no trivialization came from Mom. She understood and took it seriously from the start. She did not know about mental illness or disorders but she did know that something was wrong and that her son needed help. She was the first one to point out that her sister and her Dad and others in her family all exhibited a very similar behavior. It was so relieving to have someone know and to not be hiding my obsessions all the time. It instantly made me feel like we were now fighting the giant together. There is no way to overstate the importance of well-reasoned self-disclosure if you are to successfully battle your giants.

I discussed with Mom how I thought my aunt had what I had. From what was visible, she had many of the same "rules." Mom connected all the dots and told stories about her sister. She also shared stories about her Dad, who used to have to have his pasta cut precisely to a certain size or else he'd get very violent and exhibited a wealth of other OCD behaviors. Lastly, she told all about an uncle who hoarded all of his money to the extent that he lived in a rundown house and was unwilling to spend anything on anyone — even himself.

The first step taken toward freedom was telling Mom. The second step was realizing that this giant was OCD. As Mom stood firmly with me and with immense compassion, I began to read — and read voraciously.

The reading was aimed at learning anything and everything about OCD. Everything lined up. This diagnosis was right on the money. Virtually every obsession and every compulsion could be linked to the overarching themes that obsessive-compulsive disorder has. The symptoms were a spot on match. My OCD has, at one time or another, manifested almost all of the major themes in all of the literature and manifested some others on top of those. In other words, whereas most people seem to have a specific concentration in terms of their obsession, mine had all of them. Books on OCD were acquired and slowly gave me the knowledge to fight. Through reading, it became clear that there was just faulty wiring in my head and that none of the threats or commands were credible. None of the sanctions would happen without counting, checking, cleaning, ordering, or doing any other inane and ridiculous commands that it shouted so many times per day. This was endlessly liberating.

Reading always changed everything. Knowledge better equipped me to fight the giant. That is, understanding the giant took the fear out of it. The absurd and endless commands were not special messages, nor were they occurring to everyone else. Instead, they were a genetic anomaly in my genes that was passed on. Knowing that genes are the culprit, and not some other force, made viewing the problem of disobeying it differently. I read and talked to Mom about all of it. She was my confidant. This began to make a remarkable difference.

It enabled a scientific and rational view of OCD.

From that point on if I didn't place a piece of paper at a specific angle — toward the northwest — twenty-two times in a row (this was part of an order phase), the cherished ability to read would not be taken away. Confidence grew as disobedience grew and it became obvious that this was the case. Logic and reason became the stone and sling to slay the great Goliath that OCD had become. They were weapons. From this point forward, I would not just get thrown to the ground. I would get up stronger, like Antaeus, and fight back.

Experimentation with this new tool of fighting back began. In each and every case when fighting back was done it became clear that OCD was a liar. When I touched something and didn't get a positive thought, nothing got marred or destroyed or cursed. This was part of the good thoughts and feelings phase of OCD (never found this in textbooks). It consumed thoughts and feelings for a very long time.

During this very early period of understanding, I learned about what is the golden rule of OCD: to obey it is to make it stronger. To disobey it is to weaken it. The more logic was used and the more rebellion was used, the weaker it got. The commands came just the same. But they weren't absolutely necessary decrees like those shouted from an angry parent. Instead, they grew weaker as they were disobeyed.

Now not only did I get up off the ground when assaulted by OCD's endless commands, but was able to push the giant back. But OCD just fought back with more intense feelings of guilt, fear, and shame. Of the thousand or so commands it gave each day, I still obeyed three quarters of them – the feelings were so strong. But now I was strong enough to disobey about one quarter of them through my disobedience and disclosure.

"Mom, right now OCD is saying that I cannot eat the tomato sauce you made because the tomatoes were purchased on the same day we lost the baseball game. Therefore, it feels that if I eat the tomatoes in your sauce that will ensure that more games will be lost."

Mom smiled caringly and then laughed and shook her head, "You know how ridiculous that is, don't you, honey?"

"Yes, it is absurd and there is no connection between the tomatoes and doing poorly in a baseball game," I said honestly. "But there is no shaking the feeling, Mom. It is too strong."

"Disobey it!" She would shout in a kind way.

And I would. Stating the obsession aloud to someone trusted took a lot of the stigma out of it. I did this with Mom constantly. It was done with Mom with a lot of the obsessions that couldn't be shaken. Mom, in addition to everything else, served as my teammate against OCD. It was and is wonderful. I was no longer alone.

OCD did not back down entirely as I read, understood, and fought. It is an insidious and awful dictatorial presence. It is like a virus or a rat in that it will find a way to survive no matter what you throw at it. It began finding ways to use the very remedies that were so helpful to beat it and turned them against me.

For example, to combat the intense guilt that accompanied disobeying each command, I used my faith. OCD was viewed as giving false commands to rule life. Therefore, I thought of OCD is a false God. I argued to myself that obeying a false God is idolatry. Therefore, every time OCD's orders were disobeyed, the second commandment was being violated: *Thou shalt have no other gods.*

Now, to be clear, I am not psychotic. OCD is not a god. However, when conceived of in this way, it worked. When I thought of obeying OCD as disobeying God, it made it incredibly easier to disobey OCD. This is continued to be done to this day. During each day, you may see me making the sign of the cross and hear me muttering something similar to "I'll obey Jesus and not you," while its commands are disobeyed.

OCD began to use this method against me. Slowly, as I progressed through high school, I repeated that mantra often. All of a sudden, I began to say the mantra a specific number of times. Or, the right feeling had to be felt when saying the mantra and had to say it over and over and over until the right feeling was gotten.

OCD "saw" that I could defeat its basic mechanism with this new thought process and with Mom. Its obsessions all had compulsions. All of the compulsions could be identified and disobeyed. Therefore, OCD fought back by leaving out a compulsion to its newest onslaught of obsessions. I became a pure obsessional in addition to the thousand commands per day that had a compulsion attached to them.

A good example of this is with body image. In our remarkably superficial and empty culture, I would say that appearance — body image — becomes an obsession, or deep interest, for everyone at one time or another during their development. OCD monitors any weakness in your mind and prays on virtually anything that you care about. Its threats are almost universally about taking the things that you care about. In this way, I always viewed OCD as a sort of mafia. It holds hostage what you love and coerces you to do what it wants under threat. This is why its earliest threat was to take Mom away if I did not do what it asked. It did this endlessly and constantly over the years.

In high school, body image was no exception to OCD's mafia-esque rules. In eleventh grade, I was obsessed. The problem is that the body image obsession went far beyond the normal interest in body image. A mirror couldn't be walked by or for that matter any reflection such as a glass with something dark behind it without checking the image in it. Mirrors were checked hundreds of times per day. Checking was occurring so much because of being convinced that I perceived certain aspects of my physical self in a negative way. Image became the obsession and checking the mirror became the compulsion. Leaving class to go to the bathroom was common and checking occurred over and over each day. This is a purely obsessional aspect of OCD and met the criteria of another disorder: *Body Dysmorphic Disorder.* However, it was OCD. I checked the mirror due to a desire to confirm the awful horror of what was being felt — it seemed to be a full compulsion and a full obsession. Upon closer review, it became clear that no compulsion was needed to continue to be obsessed with image. This became the beginning of a new phase of OCD: pure obsessional.

With the advent of purely obsessional OCD, there was a certain defeat. It could not be battled in the way other obsessions connected to compulsions could be battled each day. There didn't seem to be a way to fight a pure obsession. Ignoring it doesn't work. Avoiding it doesn't work. This was when another breaking point came.

"I can't beat it anymore," I explained to Mom, crying hysterically. It was the first year of college and this was during the many nightmares experienced by bipolar disorder as well. She knew about the OCD but she did not know about the bipolar disorder.

"It's okay, honey," Mom said as she hugged me. "It's too much. We're going to get you some help now sweetheart."

The psychiatrist was a big step. It was, to Mom and Dad, a sort of desperate last resort. There were strong inroads made by knowing what it was and understanding its mechanisms. But I wasn't strong enough to disobey it all the time. And it found ways to work around the methods that were designed to beat it and were working. Life, at that time, was virtually a straitjacket of obsessions and compulsions.

The psychiatrist did two things for me.

"You have quite a case of obsessive compulsive disorder," she said as we sat in her office.

I nodded, her statement affirming what was already known. The first thing the psychiatrist did was give the label for the disorder already known. This was crucial. As social workers, we are always warned that labels are deleterious to the psyche of the patient. However, as a patient, the label provides validation and the satisfaction that you have what you believe you have. It wasn't just our opinion now. Someone with letters next to their name — someone considered credible in the medical realm — thought it, too.

The psychiatrist organized her papers as she thought about what pill she wanted to prescribe. She looked up, adjusted her glasses, and stated, "I am going to start you on Zoloft. We'll start with 75-milligrams and see how you do."

Of course, I didn't know anything about Zoloft. But this woman knew mental disorders and said that this pill would help. Her label was affirming, but did not provide a remedy. The medication provided a prospective remedy.

"Absolutely," I said and nodded eagerly.

I have taken over fifteen psychiatric medications to date. For each one, I meticulously researched everything about it, right down to the way it inhibits the synapses in the neurons. Many psychiatrists say that this is yet another facet of OCD — that I over research everything and overdo everything. I disagree. Researching everything very thoroughly does not run on the same engine as all of my obsessions and compulsions. There is no consequence if nothing is researched. It could be a pure obsession, but it seems logical to want to understand your problem as well as you possibly can.

Zoloft, like every psychiatric medication, has a long list of side effects. The "common ones" weren't worrisome but the less common ones, such as seizures and hallucinations, were a lot more concerning. With great trepidation I weighed the paralyzation that was caused by the straitjacket of OCD versus the possibility of seeing little green people in my room or whatever the pills would bring. As was the case with all fifteen psychotropics taken, it eventually became worth the risk. The risk is always small as the rare side effects occur to only a fraction of the population. So it was worth it. I took the little blue pill.

"Zoloft should help you manage some of your obsessive thoughts thereby curbing your compulsions," she said with her professorial air.

The only good thing to say for Zoloft is that it did not hurt. Only a few of the side effects affected me and they were very common and nothing that would cause its cessation. Conversely, there was no benefit derived from the drug. The best that can be said for it is that for a short time, I believed it would help conquer OCD. I thought, *I have the magic pill now, OCD can be disobeyed without any repercussions.* But it didn't. It did nothing.

As always, OCD was two steps ahead. The methods of disobedience were slowly just transforming into OCD's new rituals. In other words, the methods of disobeying it were becoming obsessions and compulsions of OCD. To give an example, let's say OCD was demanding driving only on roads that had even route numbers because any driving on the roads that had odd route numbers would result in the girl I was seeing breaking up with me. The disobedience was then — and is now — to "tell" OCD that *I will not listen to your commands; only to God's commands.* Followed by the sign of the cross.

Shortly, I began to make the sign of the cross hundreds of times per day. I did it many times when disobeying a command. Or, I'd have to repeat, "I will not listen to its commands, but only God's commands," in even numbers. It was very embarrassing in public so I had to whisper all this repeating like a ventriloquist, with no lips moving and doing it softly.

Four psychiatrists were seen in all for OCD. Four medications were taken that were specifically designed to treat it. Each was an SSRI (selective serotonin reuptake inhibitor) or an SNRI (selective norepinephrine reuptake inhibitor). The SSRIs, such as Prozac and Celexa, are for OCD as well as other psychological ailments while the SNRI Effexor was not. Using it for OCD was "off label use."

Prozac did not affect OCD in a positive way at all. It did bring with it a surge of anxiety and other side effects that were so strong I discontinued it. Celexa followed suit. It did not help at all.

The SNRI Effexor was taken to combat a different giant: bipolar depression. However, the psychiatrist agreed that it may help with OCD. It didn't help at all. During the two years on it, it had only a placebo effect.

However, the discontinuation syndrome from Effexor was by far the most brutal of any medication taken. It nearly destroyed me. Not only was it not a benefit in any way, it had an extremely negative effect.

First came the "electric shocks" that felt like the beginnings of a seizure. This happened periodically throughout the day. Next was the intense nausea that came in pretty much any a social situation. If there were people, there was the nausea. The feeling was so strong that I had to leave constantly to go to the bathroom to gag. This occurred for nine-and-a-half months after taking that so-called medication. Sitting in classes or at work, the anxiety of the social world brought a surge of nausea. It would continue to grow and grow until leaving was necessary. The fear of vomiting in that social world always made me leave. The worst part was that nothing worked to ease it or cure it. Chipping off pieces of ginger root and drinking them was a remedy that was tried. There was a litany of other remedies tried. Coming late, coming early, and distracting my thoughts in social situations were a few methods tried. But nothing worked.

The last ditch effort before quitting everything was to purge my body of the last chemical being used that affects neurotransmitters. Caffeine was the number one vice. Coffee seemed to give the ability to continue to get off the ground because it lifted from the fog of depression for a short time. Coffee affected the neurotransmitter adenosine and the hope was that adenosine was involved with whatever Effexor did to me. The cessation from coffee had a miraculous result. In November 2009, after nine months of having to avoid or leave every single social situation other than those with family (because there was no anxiety with them), it stopped. It stopped when all caffeine intake stopped.

OCD wrapped itself around even the side effects of a medication used to treat it. It is like a great python that wraps itself around anything the sufferer cares about. It intertwines itself around everything and anything it can and suffocates its sufferer with fear and ritual. It targets any thought of fear and uses that fear to get you to do whatever ritual it wants.

To this day, caffeine is terrifying due to whatever Effexor did. Caffeine, since November 2009, remains the cornerstone of contamination fears. Exorbitant anxiety dominates my consciousness whenever it is around me or in proximity to things I care about. Tanya, for instance, had a "coffee station" in a separate and isolated part of the kitchen in our first apartment and currently has one in our house. If someone is drinking coffee and touches something of mine, whatever was touched has to be washed or thrown away. OCD has made caffeine for me into what germs are to most people with contamination issues. The problem is that the regular germ issues are ever present, too.

Whatever way OCD manifested itself over the years, the bottom line is that medications did not work a bit for me. It did not make me stronger against the great giant of OCD. Psychiatrists wanted to abandon SSRIs because they had no effect. We talked about tricyclic medications, which were abandoned years ago because the side effects are often so much more severe than SSRIs. I respectfully declined. To this day, I have taken a little more than half of the FDA approved drugs for OCD. I have no intention to take anymore.

Psychotherapy was the next weapon. One of OCD's little tricks was to demand silence. This clandestine nature of OCD helps keep it alive in the same way the little boy not talking to his parents about the boogeyman under his bed helps keep the boogeyman alive. Therefore, I decided to go headlong into psychotherapy for OCD as well as for the other mental giants that have made consciousness so difficult. This was, undoubtedly, the most effective of the professional treatments tried for OCD. The endless commands that were received from OCD on a daily basis were explained zealously in every session. These commands were categorized into themes such as repeating, hoarding, doubting/checking, contamination, counting, pure obsession, and so on. We discussed whatever obsession was at the forefront at that given time and my feelings and frustrations. Psychotherapy was genuinely helpful. That is, it was extremely helpful to talk through it with a trained professional. It was good for to hear how absurd the obsessions and compulsions were from someone other than Mom.

But there was still no solution in sight. The psychotherapist could listen all day but listening did not make it stop. It felt good but it did not make me stronger. Then the psychotherapist recommended a few books and reinforced the behavior from those books in session. I read them at once and once again reading truly illuminated the best path. *Brain Lock* by Brian Schwartz and *Overcoming Obsession* by Foa and Wilson are still the long time go-to resources because they, along with reason, provided the strategic map for how I have become stronger through this daily battle with OCD. It was through reason and self-education that it became possible to finally get up off the ground long enough to get stronger to battle OCD.

The premise was simple. The psychotherapist would sit and drink his tea across from my chair, which made me very tense, of course, due to the caffeine lurking just a few feet away. He would say it was not caffeinated, but the cup that he drank it in had caffeinated tea in it regularly. That was enough to cause anxiety.

"First, identify the obsession," I would say, echoing both the books and the psychotherapist's instruction.

"Just like you identify some of them each and every week in here, Kurt," he affirmed.

"Second, call the obsession what it is: an obsession. It is the result of faulty wiring, a misfiring of neurotransmitters, and its endless threats are not real."

"That's it," he encouraged, "so when you have the compulsion to buy two shirts because the first shirt is an odd numbered shirt and your mind tells you that only even is good, simply acknowledge that it is OCD talking. OCD is very real, but it is not telling you the truth."

"Right." Personifying OCD and using that personification to overcome it was something learned at a young age. The third step was very foreign to me. "The third and final step is to simply do something else, something other than the compulsion."

"That's it!" He would nod encouragingly. "Just do something else."

We probably had variations of this conversation over a thousand times in his office over the two and a half years of our weekly sessions. It was gone over another hundred times each and every day and done constantly. There was something about having Mom, him, and authors Foa, Wilson, and Schwartz alongside me that gave strength to fight harder. I viewed OCD in much the same way and did much the same things in the past, when I identified it and read about it. But there was something about the fact that we codified a creed, as a team, to fight it together that was incredibly helpful. Also, the fact that the man a few feet away understood what I was battling against made a tremendous difference.

I was trying to fight it before — to destroy it. The psychotherapist and the books taught that this is the wrong approach — and an approach that will, ironically, make OCD stronger. The key, they said, was to see it and not fight it. The treatment was to simply nod to it, acknowledge it, and do something else.

Psychotherapy was, by far, the best professional treatment for OCD. I hardly walked out cured. I was being thrown to the ground every bit as much every day when walking out of psychotherapy as when walking in. However, the psychotherapist taught that these obsessions will likely always be there. He taught that the harder these obsessions were fought, the stronger they became. And seeing that was invaluable.

Overcoming OCD is a lifelong learning experience. Learning that it will always be with me and that fighting or suppressing the thoughts only makes them stronger were great tools given by the psychotherapist and those wonderful books. Having Schwartz's, Foa's and Wilson's methods of identifying the obsession, acknowledging it as OCD, and doing something else was the new game plan. But something was missing. Every day the enormous giant that is OCD continued to be overwhelming.

That's when the opportunity came to add a personal touch to it. As noted, I am zealous about English literature and writing. I applied some of the literary tools gained from all the readings done to battle OCD. In particular, personification was used even more zealously than in the past. This means personifying OCD and giving it human attributes and making it my own "mortal enemy." Many psychiatrists, upon hearing this, would classify this approach as "psychotic." But it's not. OCD is not actually a person, but it can helpful to think of it that way to overcome it.

OCD is one of those giants who would throw Antaeus to the ground. Each day is a wrestling match where OCD is like a thousand giants coming to challenge me one after the other. Each one — each obsessive impulse — psychologically hurls me to the ground. But there is no defeat and no staying down. Around a thousand times per day I will get up and then hear the giant's commands but refuse to obey them.

And this is what makes OCD shrivel up. It becomes weaker with disobedience. The giant is beaten by hearing it but not listening to it. The giant's only power is the fear given to it via the compulsions that seem unstoppable. Through disobedience, it shrivels and dies.

This personification proved to be a very valuable tool. It worked more than psychotherapy, more than medication, and more than the fear of becoming Howard Hughes. This mindset changed my thinking about OCD much like reading did. Between reading, personification, and openly talking about OCD, this giant is not allowed to ever consume me completely. It never stops trying and it likely never will stop trying. But I am armed with a sort of civil disobedience learned from Thoreau, Gandhi, Tolstoy, and, above all, Christ.

This is not to say that every day is not a struggle. It is. OCD never stops. It especially never stops trying to find new obsessions and compulsions to take over your life. You are deluged with fear and orders and commands to do things very specific ways. Yes, it is caused by some anomaly in genes, but these are your genes. And it is very clear that OCD will never stop as long as this brain is conscious.

It is important to note that the pure obsessions, which started with body dysmorphic disorder, continue to be the greatest struggle. If obsessions come without a clear compulsion, they are infinitely harder to beat back. In psychotherapy and in books, there is always that incredible model that works for me. I identify the obsession, acknowledge it for what it is (OCD), and do something else. Don't give it attention. It is so simple, but so potent, a tool.

For example, I played baseball for fourteen years as a pitcher, a shortstop, and a third baseman. In ninth grade, when the pressure was on during tryouts, I could no longer throw the baseball straight. I literally threw it directly into the ground or way above the target or very wildly to either side. The obsessions became how to throw the baseball straight.

It was one of the most embarrassing moments when the high school baseball coach announced, "Every time the ball hits the floor while you're playing catch everyone does steps!" This meant the entire team would be forced to run up and down steps at a very fast pace if the ball hit the ground. The pressure was like pouring gasoline on the obsession of how to throw the ball straight. Ball after ball was thrown into the stands and into the ground. All of the players were lined up directly across from each other and the task was simply to throw the ball straight to one another. It was beyond humiliating. That was the last time I played in that league.

This obsession could not be beaten. Every time I picked up the baseball there was a fierce obsession on when to let it go, where to position each limb, and how to make it go straight. It was not known then, but this was a pure obsession. It is, in its own way, the most damaging type of obsession. It almost always arises out of very stressful situations. It is battled in much the same way as all of the other obsessions, except it wins occasionally. It wins when doing something else means quitting baseball or something else that is cared about.

But by and large, fighting back successfully can be learned through understanding and intervention. This makes all the difference. Every day is another installment of this epic war. Constant battles are lost in that war. But this war will be won. I am made stronger by resisting OCD's fear tactics more often than not. I continue to change the commands and obsessions through different forms of resistance as OCD revises its battle plan constantly. It weakens when it is disobeyed. It gets stronger when it is obeyed. This is the only thing that is for certain in our battle.

It is one thing to learn to battle OCD, it is quite another to become stronger by battling it. Most people would not argue that either boxer in a fight is made stronger by getting hit. However, the daily battle with OCD does make me stronger.

First, the tolerance for constant adversity that it creates is immense. Getting flooded with obsessions and having to battle them is something that prepares you to deal with adversity each and every day. Second, OCD innately bestows certain gifts. People with OCD tend to be very focused and very driven. The OCD creates this drive. Organization becomes a great strength.

OCD also instills an epic fear of failure due to the perfectionism that often accompanies it. Also, because everything is thought about obsessively, everything is thought about very deeply.

And perhaps the greatest asset gained from OCD is the ability to critically think. OCD was and is one of the greatest factors in the continued development of my ability to critically think. Around one thousand times per day decisions have to be made about whether to obey or to disobey OCD. Critical thinking is what allows disobedience. OCD is constantly developing critical thinking abilities. It is through critical thinking that its lies are revealed.

If this perverse puppeteer were left to just run rampant, my fate would be very similar to Howard Hughes (without the wealth and celebrity, of course). A very, very solitary life would be necessary so its rules could be followed without interruption (Tanya, for instance, does many things that drives OCD crazy). Special utensils would be used that can only touch certain foods. Hand sanitizer and many bottles of liquid soap would be everywhere. In each room, there would be a requirement to step a certain number of footsteps. No clothes that "something good happened in" would be thrown or given away — ever. There would be even numbers of everything, from toasters to chairs. Everything would be ordered perfectly and meticulously and there would be large meltdowns if anything was touched.

And it would get worse — so much worse.

However, this is not the future. Howard Hughes will not be the future. OCD will throw down this consciousness via obsessions and compulsions every day. But a steady stream of strength will come as it is resisted.

Strength will come from being thrown to the ground by it and getting up and not being intimidated or defeated.

Strength will come with the critical thinking that it takes to disobey its compulsions.

Strength will come with surviving it.

Strength will come by reading the latest treatments and understanding the neurological basis of OCD.

Strength will come.

IV

BACK PROBLEMS

ON JANUARY 20, 2009, I got knocked down again. It was the fifth month of the first job since the brain injury. I was very nervous and very eager to prove myself in this job. I ran a small program that delivered and set up furniture to the apartments of individuals who suffered from mental illness. It seemed a great fit and, quite frankly, I couldn't believe I was being asked to do it since disclosing all of the limitations I had disclosed to the supervisor.

I wanted to do it perfectly — OCD style.

To help move all this furniture was a minimum wage paid group of guys who worked hard and were very helpful. They all suffered from severe mental health issues. The program was an employment program for individuals suffering from severe mental health issues made to benefit (to deliver furniture to) individuals with severe mental health issues. Therefore, many had some attendance issues and didn't need the money because they had few expenses, had SSI, and were getting other help from the agency. Others had a great deal of work limitations, both physical and mental. There was only two or three — maximum — helping do it at any time. This is because no more could fit in the truck.

Bipolar disorder caused tremendous socially anxiety for the vast majority of the time that was spent at this job. It was excruciating to go in each day. I sweated, felt nauseous, was incredibly socially anxious, and was very forgetful. Needless to say, assertiveness was not an obvious strength of mine. And that is how I ended up on the other side of every single piece of furniture for the first four months.

Every day I was on one side of lifting pretty much every piece of furniture, piece after piece, day after day. I lifted far too much. Each day I returned to a tiny efficiency in Binghamton with what felt like a fire burning in my back. It was as if the day's work resulted in someone pouring a bag of fire ants into the muscles of my back where they furiously bit all night and day. I convinced myself that this was just part of doing hard physical labor — of "being a man" as Dad would say — and didn't let it stop me.

Other romanticized images of machismo and grace under pressure factored into my thought process to continually push to go on despite the pain.

However, the overarching factor that kept me pushing was the fact that this was the first time working competitively since the brain injury six years ago. There was no failing — failing would ensure SSI was my income forever and would cripple an already severely wounded confidence. The last competitive job I held (pre brain injury) was as a produce stock worker at a local supermarket. Since then, doctors said future employment, if at all, would likely be a sheltered workshop. It was a point of pride, dignity, and survival to push on.

I was also pushing myself in other ways. The only other friend that I had other than Angelo during this time was a college acquaintance who liked to have intellectual conversations while getting drunk. He asked to help him move and I did. He used me as a one-man moving crew for all of his belongings. It was with him and another acquaintance that I engaged other strenuous activities including racquetball, football, and other sports. This likely helped to further the exhaustion of the back muscles.

On January 26, 2009, my body had had enough. I was trying to type at my desk on a Sunday morning. I'll never forget the moment that my whole body just froze. It was as if my tired and weary arms got stuck in the ice that the back became after all that lifting. All of the upper back muscles just seemed to seize up and go on strike all at once. In one horrible instant, bending down to pick things up was no longer possible. Only very lightweight objects could be picked up without great pain. I never experienced anything like it and was very scared.

A flood of exquisite and horrifying panic washed over my entire body. My car keys could be picked up off of the table only by bending at the knees in order not to move my nearly paralyzed arms. It took a Herculean effort to conjure up enough movement amidst the pain to drive two or three blocks to the nearby emergency room.

"My back just froze!" I told the people at the front desk of the emergency room. "I have incredibly limited movement of my arms."

"Okay, have a seat," the unimpressed worker stated.

I sat there in utter fear and focused only on the worst possible scenarios. I feared that these frozen arms would never loosen up. I feared being crippled physically in addition to the mental slings and arrows that were constantly crippling me.

"Kurt Warner?" the emergency room worker called back.

"You stated you are having back pain?" she asked.

Everything was answered honestly and truly. However, the answers were hurried and upset due to no sleep the night before or the night before that. I tried to describe it accurately enough so that they would solve it.

A few x-rays later, a diagnosis of "myofascial strain" was given. A prescription for two muscle relaxants was given. The muscle relaxants were taken and a hot bath was also taken because the warm water was all that was soothing. I prayed that my body would rebound and be better in the morning.

Almost nothing was better from the medication. Slightly more mobility was gained over the night but the upper back, where the arms connect to the back, was throbbing and in incredible pain. They could not be extended outwardly to do anything. The only way they were usable was by keeping the elbows against the body and just use the forearms. If the elbows were extended further from my body, the aching and throbbing pain began. Any movement geared toward lifting felt like it was pulling the limbs out of their sockets. The pain made me tremble – literally. There was also a burning sensation that felt as if a hot poker was being shoved in me. On top of this, it was hard to stand for long periods. My legs felt like jelly and the discomfort forced sitting down and ankles felt like they were going to cave in on themselves. Walking was still easy, though, so, this was not yet a major concern. There were enough somatic issues to deal with at the time.

All focus remained entirely on the upper back. After January 26, 2009, it was impossible to even sit at the desk and write. Writing was life-sustaining and so this was incredibly devastating. For months, any writing was performed by sitting on the couch in the tiny apartment with a journal on my lap and tears welling up. It was not the same.

My supervisor was tremendously understanding.

"Something happened to my back over the weekend."

"What happened?" he asked.

A very brief synopsis was given.

"Well," he said, "take it easy if you can come in to work. Have the other guys lift all of the furniture until you get better. If you are able to come in you can just do what you can."

I did just as he asked. Everything possible was done. Being in such a severe depression during much of this period, it was only through adrenaline and fear that I got anything done. It was due to the extremely hard work, compassion, and dedication of the other workers that everything else got done. When I had to tell the other guys on the truck that they would have to do all the lifting from then on, I was incredibly anxious. The plan was to take the closest guy to me aside. He was a big guy who was full of kindness and had an even bigger personality. He was open and honest and kind and sensitive and it was great having him in the truck. He knew the job inside and out and helped immensely when I started. I'll never forget approaching him first,

"Steve, I have some bad news."

"Yeah what's going on?" Steve asked concernedly.

"Well, my back just froze up over the weekend. I was in the emergency room and will not be able to lift anything. Can you help get the other guys to pick up the slack?"

Steve was very capable and very confident. He took the statement as a vote of confidence in him and it affirmed to him that he was copilot.

"Of course," he said.

The others did not like that I did not move furniture with them and that they had to pick up the slack. It felt humiliating each and every day and felt very awkward when not moving furniture while they did. They did not like it but I simply could not do it.

The ER stated that it was, indeed, "myofascial strain." I would be back to lifting in at most a few weeks. This was the assumption.

It was wrong. First, the pain went on for a month. Then it went on for two months. Panic ensued. There were an endless amount of hot baths, muscle relaxants, and a myriad of exercises, and I even enrolled in physical therapy. And, of course, I read anything and everything on the back. Reading always remained the best weapon against any ailment.

But nothing helped. It got a little better from the original insult. The arms were not frozen in pain anymore. I could not move them in any direction without pain. But the second any activity was tried wherein they were extended outwardly at all, therein came a remarkable burning and acidic feeling that ended the attempt. Lifting was absolutely impossible. Typing was torture.

Ten months of physical therapy did nothing. In addition, I went swimming three times per week because when swimming, nothing hurt and the belief was that it just had to be helping. But swimming did not make anything better. I took every pill that any credible person stated would help and took everything and did everything that would help arthritis, bulging discs, and other back maladies that it could possibly be. That was the major issue: There was no name for it. There was no diagnosis.

That's when an appointment was made to see the neurosurgeon who saved my life. He also specialized in back problems. And, everything that he said was trusted.

"I'm not sure what is," he said as he looked on with his kind, compassionate face. "It could be a lot of things and the only way I'm going to know what it is if imaging is taken."

"Well, I'll do whatever it takes."

He smiled. "Well, your CAT scan shows nothing abnormal. I am not willing to give you any kind of imaging tests with the dye injected into your arteries because you have complications with your arteries."

"Okay. But isn't there anything else besides the CAT scan that will show you what it looks like in there?"

"Yes, there is. An MRI would give the best view. However, I'm not willing to give you that yet."

"Why?"

"You have a titanium clip in your brain. That is safe to put through an MRI, but there are some risks. Your back pain will probably clear up within a few months. If it persists, I would be willing to do the MRI," he said honestly, "but if we can avoid it, we should. There is a small chance that the heat vacuum could suck that titanium clip off of your artery."

MRI stands for magnetic resonance imaging. It uses an incredibly powerful magnet to create an image of the inside of your body.

This was the only conversation with the late neurosurgeon who saved me that was about getting an MRI. Everything he said was listened to and that meant MRIs were off the table.

A CAT scan is easy. It consists of lying on an open table for five minutes or so. I've gotten hundreds of these. In addition to Dr. Sedor not finding any problems with the CAT scan, it was taken to other back specialists who also found nothing wrong with it.

"Does that mean I can't get a diagnosis for this pain?"

"It means that based on CAT scans you will not get a diagnosis. There's nothing wrong with your CAT scan. My advice to you is to give it time and we will see how you do," Dr. Sedor replied.

I did just that. However, as time was given, my wonderful neurosurgeon passed away. Therefore, there would be no trusted and tested neurosurgeon who truly new the totality of the situation to help make the right decisions for treatment.

As the back was given plenty of time to heal, ways to work around it were figured out. The first priority was work.

At the point where the arms connect into the back there was — and is still — such pain. The pain was so great at first virtually everything done with the arms caused severe pain and burning in the back. My hand couldn't be put on top of the steering wheel because the burning was so bad.

Lifting felt like my arms were being pulled out of my body. There was so much pain it prevented lifting even a folding chair in the first few months.

How, then, could a job be maintained that requires lifting furniture into a truck, driving it to be delivered, delivering it, and setting it up people's homes?

First, the aforementioned boss and friend was told

about the situation. He is a very reasonable man. A policy of being completely upfront with him was maintained.

Second, social anxiety has to be mitigated. A large part of the reason the injury was sustained was due to an inability to confront the employees about not being involved in lifting everything. Learning to stop caring what they may think of me was practiced constantly. I worked furiously to change the entrenched thought process that put so much emphasis on the opinion of the other person.

Third, a strategy was developed with the workers. Steve was the copilot and he was given responsibility for deflecting some of the heat for unpopular decisions. This paid off. Steve used his very deep voice to push the other workers whenever they would ask why I wasn't helping them with the furniture. Honesty was also employed in that the back injury was explained to the crew, some of whom were understanding and some who were not quite as understanding.

Nevertheless, every day was agonizing and remarkably socially anxious. Embarrassment and shame were omnipresent and self-hated was felt every moment on that truck after the back froze up.

Six months went by like this. The guys in the truck did an incredible job and all the work got done. A lot of time was spent recruiting more and more labor so that it would not become an issue when some of the guys inevitably left. Every facet of the program was transformed or slightly altered. But again, a world was created that could be managed and worked around.

The unrelenting social anxiety, the never healing back pain, the endless OCD, and the cruel bipolar disorder were eventually too much. After six more months, a resignation letter was typed and handed in to Angelo, who did not expect it. The premise behind the letter was that the back simply needed pure rest to heal.

The letter was handed in with embarrassment and shame.

"I'm leaving — quitting,"

"No, you're not," Angelo replied assuredly.

"I have to!" I said and explained the back condition to him again.

"You've done a better job with that program than anyone ever has," he said. "You are a very valuable part of our team. So before you quit, why don't you just take some time to rest and heal your back?"

Rest. This notion sounded wonderful. Maybe with no stress — physical or social — the back would get better. I did as he asked.

But nothing got better. I stayed in the tiny efficiency apartment in Binghamton and hardly came out. Absolutely nothing was done that would aggravated the back insofar as possible. Eating well and sleeping well were top priorities. All kinds of dietary supplements were ingested such as calcium and magnesium and logs were kept of everything taken and everything done. Immense amount of liquids were imbibed each day. Muscles were stretched every half hour. Topical numbing gels were used around-the-clock, not because they eliminated the pain, but because the cool sensation distracted the pain in the slightest bit. Immense reading was done that was focused on ways to treat it and to diagnose it by using the pain as the guide.

Nothing helped. Everything done was useless, a lot like everything initially done in an attempt to stop the formidable bipolar cycles. Suffering was just the same no matter what new intervention was implemented. The things tried only helped insofar as the modicum of hope that they gave when they were being tried. Like so many of the treatments for OCD and so many of the treatments for bipolar, it was endlessly disheartening.

After a few months off, there was a call from the agency. My supervisor asked if I wanted a new job. It was a job coordinating a housing program for individuals suffering chemical dependency issues.

At the time he offered this job, no more than a line or two could be typed without intense pain in the upper back. It did not hurt nearly as badly as when it first froze, but it still limited every activity that was engaged in and was extremely painful and frustrating.

Writing, for instance, always remained one of my greatest aids. Never was a day missed of journaling. It was absolutely devastating that I could no longer sit at a desk and write, though. Now, a journal was set on my lap and everything was written that way.

How, then, could this new job possibly be taken on

while not being able to stand for any significant duration, legs turn into jelly when on my feet, being unable to type without tears forming from pain, and being unable to lift anything more than five pounds?

I will never forget discussing this with Mom. It was a critical conversation. It was very clear that this existence of mine would be significantly impacted by its outcome. To make matters more arduous, a crippling depression dominated and darkened my consciousness and dampened the ability to do much of anything. It was also around the seventh month of the cessation from Effexor. This meant every time I was around unfamiliar people, a very strong and overwhelming nausea came — think *A Clockwork Orange* only with the sickness coming from people rather than violence. At this point, every emphasis was put on figuring out any way to get through life that did not involve suicide. During our conversation, I couldn't stand my own skin and the anxiety of the depression and the decision enveloped me. I paced up and down the hallway and was nervous and erratic.

"I just don't know how I could possibly do it, Ma."

"You will find a way," she replied. "You can do whatever you want, honey, but this seems like a great opportunity. It's worth a shot. What do you have to lose?"

That was her thesis: *what could be the harm? what could be lost by trying?* She believed that I should just try it — nothing more. She put no pressure on either way. But she argued that it was a wonderful opportunity and that maybe it would work out. If not, then so what?

I felt very differently. If it was tried it but failed, there was no getting back up again. It was highly unlikely that there would ever be another opportunity to run a program with this supervisor — with someone who cared and understood a lot about the situation. This was as good as it gets. And if this could not be achieved, then I might as well get lots of tuna fish and Ramen and start living under that bridge.

In the end, Mom and I decided that it was the most reasonable conclusion to take a leap of faith and give it a go. I was betting everything on the idea that the back would heal and that the nausea, social anxiety, and depressions could become navigable if ways were figured out to work around them.

This decision was made with one caveat. When the back froze up in January, within twelve hours I was sitting in a chair with the shotgun in my mouth. I was making positive that the pain was not so great that the gun couldn't be angled to hit the "right spot." The decision was made then and there that if this job failed, it was over.

Every day was a Herculean struggle just to get through the day and back to sleep. My confidence could not be more abysmal and it was hard to find even one job that was practical and manageable and that could be done despite the disabilities. Life was seen as nothing but a burden and a cursed responsibility to carry on in the darkness. Each and every breath was loathsome. The belief that was clung to was that it was a debt to God and Mom to keep trying, though. But there had to be a limit to how much could be withstood. The job was that limit. That was the caveat. The job was that line in the sand.

A manual from New York State was handed to me and it read *OASAS* at the top. From that, a state-funded program was to be erected out of thin air. The manual was very well laid out. It gave me lots of freedom to compose the program the way I saw fit. It was taken home and the blueprints for the program were laid out. It was studied and help was needed to concentrate on it because such a severe and disabling depression gripped me.

On a conceptual basis, it seemed easy.

In practicality, it was torture.

The office provided was stationed at the halfway house with six full-time employees and twenty residents. My social anxiety got another trial by fire and it was truly excruciating. The office for the program was a tiny room upstairs that was previously used as a storage closet. It was here that the program was put and it was here that the vast majority of my minutes were spent. It was three walls, a door, and the smallest square window that could not be opened. For six to nine months at a stretch, I seldom mingled with anyone unless forced to by work responsibilities.

One time one of the residents remarked, "Hey, Kurt, they finally let you out your cage?"

Approximately ten months after the back injury is when this job began. However, the back pain remained excruciating. It was great fortune to get a desk with a sliding drawer below it rather than have a desk with a keyboard on top of the desk. This made typing about fifty percent easier because my arms were so low and the lower they were kept, the less pain there was. It is the lowness of the arms and the closer they are to body that make activities with them hurt much less. If they are extended straight out, or they are positioned high, the aching and burning nightmare begins.

It became clear through the manual that the job was this: to find five — and later ten — people who meet very specific criteria. Then these people were put into an apartment of their choosing but also that were under strict rent limits and up to code. Next, I was charged with helping them get an income, usually what is called temporary assistance in New York. Then, the program paid a portion of the rent from the State dollars and they paid the rest with their income. The program then helped them find employment and fostered independence. Once this was achieved, the resident had much more income and was occupied with employment. Consequently, they paid a higher portion of the rent. Ideally, and in most cases they worked and paid their portion of the rent from their employment income.

In some ways, my job became helping people become like Antaeus. I became a strong advocate of the employment piece because that is how they become like Antaeus; that is how they became stronger and more capable and independent. My program became known as the "employment program."

I did not tell anyone that every day was excruciating due to typing. But it was. Each day I felt tears the pain was so overwhelming. Typing was dreaded and was done as little as possible. The bright side, if there was a bright side, was that the job never required standing in any way. But the bright side was constantly overshadowed by the immobilizing pain that was caused by a condition I could not even get diagnosed.

Each resident met with me at least once per week. The social anxiety of these meetings actually became preferable to the pain of sitting in my office and typing out a two-page progress note after every single meeting.

"How's it going?" my boss would ask routinely.

"It's fine. I'm focusing on the employment aspect of the job. It is very unique. Most of these people can work and really do well with it. And I am happy to report that one hundred percent of them are working and paying a portion of the rent."

Then, after our talk, I'd go outside and a little, very harsh Italian cigar was lighted. The very small, incredibly pungent, thick smoke ensured the surest way a slow and methodical suicide could be committed. By smoking and inhaling the cigar, I believed I could not be held accountable for my eventual deterioration of health; after all, cigars were socially acceptable. In between appointments, I was constantly inhaling the potent little Italian cigars.

It was truly brutal to go to work each day. Between the back pain, the bipolar disorder, the OCD, and poor memory each and every day was a daily onslaught of suffering. Pleasure had no part in life and it was painful to hear people who believed it did. Every single day was a passionate search for easement to all this pain.

There were two initial and creative ways that had to be found to address the pain from the undiagnosed back pain that encumbered movement.

The first was that desk with the lowered keyboard drawer. This alone saved the job and enabled limping along for many months. Each and every day I got tears from the pain of typing. This lowered drawer still brought the tears but it took, let's say, twice the amount of time for them to come than typing without the drawer.

The second was a high backed chair. I discovered that the higher the office chair was, the better off I was. Something about having my back pressed up against the chair, like a brace, helped ease the pain. I noted this outside of work.

I remember approaching the supervisor. "Can I get a new chair?"

"What's wrong with the one you have?" he asked.

"Nothing, but it's very bad for me. Since the back problem, it really hurts to type in it. A high backed chair eases the pain a fair amount," I said with the air of a plea rather than a declarative remark.

"Go ahead," he said. He was always willing to accommodate any employee who had an issue. That was one of the reasons I went with the job. He would be compassionate whereas many other supervisors would not be.

That is how I got a high backed chair. This chair was used until the end of the job and was wonderful and helped immensely. I used the same desk that came with the lower keyboard drawer because it was lower than normal desks. As with everything, OCD created rituals around the chair and desk. I pushed and pulled the chair back and forth to get it into the "exact spot" that OCD needed it to be before going home each night, which sometimes took thirty minutes or more. The arms of the chair were ruined over many years of doing this.

However, these two improvements — a desk and a chair — enabled getting off the ground due to the back injury in these early days. However, each day was still spent in a great deal of physical pain.

There was never an end to searching for a solution. I went to many, many medical professionals — and to nonmedical ones, too. Pain killing patches were tried, other muscle relaxants were tried, narcotics were tried, an onslaught of anti-inflammatories was taken, and many other drugs were used to kill the pain. Deep tissue laser treatments were tried as were a battery of other tests such as EMGs. I tried heat and tried cold. A gym membership was purchased and strengthening was tried. Three nights per week for at least an hour was spent swimming.

Acupuncture was tried. I lived near an acupuncturist and began getting it done. I got on a table and watched this pleasant and kind little man put little needles into me. Each poke was almost painless. He would talk the whole time.

"Is that okay?"

"Yes, no problems. Can I ask you though, why are you choosing the spots you are choosing to put the needles?"

"Of course," he said. "I am putting them where you are likely to have blocked *qi*," he said, pronouncing it "chee."

"So, then, the hypothesis of acupuncture is that when qi gets blocked, putting little needles into those areas will unblock it?

"Precisely," he said happily. "And it is proven. It has been proven for thousands of years. It can cure almost any ailment."

That may be. But it didn't do anything for me. I went to see two different acupuncturists on this promise. And I have plenty of problems to be cured. I derived no benefit from it.

Another alternative medicine tried was *reiki*. Since the medical profession could not even offer a diagnosis without taking a chance on pulling a clip from my artery, all of the alternative medicine I could find was tried.

One practitioner has the treatments in his home.

"Your *chakras* are out of balance," he said as he examined different parts of the chest, neck, and abdomen. "I will be able to rebalance the chakras, I hope, and your back may improve."

This was the idea. A person's hands can scan for an imbalance of chakras, which have to do with energy. By placing their hands on certain areas, they can attempt to rebalance these chakras.

This was only done twice. It provided no relief.

Desperation oscillated me back and forth between therapies. I had one medical therapy that was long-standing and one alternative therapy that was long-standing but no real relief.

Two rounds of physical therapy were done. Both lasted about six months, so altogether physical therapy for back pain was done for about a year. This is longer than it took to relearn how to walk in physical therapy. The physical therapy for back pain was done after work and that extended the nightmarish days to nine or ten hours. This did not include all of the "exercises" that were asked to do at home. Both clinics were the same. The therapists were falsely cheery and optimistic in tone. However, it was clear that I was just another piece in their assembly line and just another hour that they were trying to get through in their day.

"What is the purpose? What are you trying to do?" I asked the tall, lanky male physical therapist with what seemed like an everlasting smile tattooed on his face.

"Strengthen your muscles around whatever vertebrae are bothering you. If we can strengthen them, that should help to reduce your pain," he said genuinely.

It sounded simple enough. Physical therapists helped me to walk again after the brain injury and I put a lot of trust in them. Absolutely everything they asked was done.

"Here's your homework," every physical therapist said at the end of every session. Each one of them would give a few papers that, I got the impression, were given to everyone with a similar ailment. The papers had figures on them doing exercises. The sheets indicated how often to do each exercise.

And all the exercises were done. The five pound weight and therapy bands were purchased and, and the exercises were performed religiously. Each appointment, then, generally consisted of showing the therapist how I was doing the exercises on the paper.

There was no benefit from any exercise that was ever given for back pain. The appointments became very cumbersome after a few months. I hated them and only went to a second long round of physical therapy because it is what every doctor suggested and it seemed like a different clinic may do it differently. They didn't.

The longest standing alternative medicine treatment was chiropractic. A classmate in graduate school said that they had a chiropractor who was absolutely amazing. The idea of someone pressing on bones in order to affect some physical change in them was horrible. But what choice was there? Nothing else was working. And my classmate stood and swore that chiropractic had cured her of a severe back issue.

There was only one chiropractor seen in my life before this one. He treated me one time. That chiropractor used my arms and with one movement — one swift twist it felt — and sounded, like he cracked every joint in the back. It did not reduce pain in the least. It seemed like a parlor trick.

For about three straight years, thirty-five minutes

were traveled at least twice and much of the time more than twice per week to see a new, highly recommended chiropractor. His office was originally set up in a professional clinic with other professionals. This gave the illusion of professionalism. But within a year, he had a falling out with the clinic and I was traveling to his personal residence to get chiropractic work done. The catch, however, was that it was not solely his residence. It was his mother's house.

"Don't bring him in the front door!" she screamed in the background. In three full years of seeing this chiropractor, she only made a physical appearance twice. But many of the "sessions" revolved around not disturbing her.

The chiropractor was a painfully emaciated man. He required payment in cash and asked only about double what the co-pay was for anything else.

"Chiropractors scare me."

"Well I don't think you will be afraid of my chiropractic technique," he said. This was in the clinic with the smell of intoxicating Chinese herbs wafting through the air.

"Why?"

"I'm very different from most chiropractors. Almost all chiropractors today do what's called a 'golden roll' technique where they manipulate many of your vertebrae at one time. I don't. I do Gonstead chiropractic. This means that I manipulate only the vertebrae that need it. I do nothing more. It is much safer."

This logic was satisfying and Gonstead chiropractic turned out to be a real and legitimate style. It was true. Proof was also provided that he was trained, that is, I required him to physically show his degree in chiropractic. After he did that, he manipulated me regularly.

He put me on a table each visit. He had two tables: one that was like an extremely thin bed and another that you had to kneel in front of and put your arms through holes and rest your body on it. That table looked like it was preparing you for the guillotine. Usually, I lay on the first table with arms underneath me. He would meticulously feel each vertebrae one after the other.

What was remarkable is that without ever saying it, he always knew — by touch — the exact vertebrae that were giving the pain. He would then focus on that area. He would take ten minutes to massage the muscle around it. Then, there was a request to breathe deeply and exhale. On one exhale, he would apply downward force — and usually a twist. There would be a very loud crunching sound. After that, great pleasure was felt. This had to be the right track.

The table that looked like it was from the Middle Ages was used as well. I would kneel and put my arms into holes in the table. He would stand above and it was the most vulnerable position ever — too vulnerable. It felt horrifying, like serial killer's torture device. But desperation will make you do anything to feel hope. And it worked out – he was able to use a different angle on that table and it cracked my back in different ways.

"How long until you believe it will make a difference in my back pain?"

"Each time you are manipulated, the bone is moving one-eighth of an inch," he said confidently. It's it is hard to say how long but if you keep getting it done, it should correct the issue."

I heard the echoes of a charlatan in his voice the entire time I went to him. But nothing else worked and this genuinely gave at least the illusion of progress. I went three times a week, then twice, and then once a week. Due to monetary concerns and the fact that there was no remarkable improvement, the appointments became every two weeks.

This is not to say that it did not help at all. Whether it was the body healing, or his treatments, it did get a little better during the time. But within a few hours it would hurt just the same as before and I almost decided to stop seeing him.

But there were certain aspects of the pain — like the inability to sit up without pain radiating throughout — did vanish. Perhaps it got better on its own, though. It is impossible to say.

Whereas it is only probable that he helped, he definitely hurt. When he hurt me, it was three years into treatment. Because it wasn't really helping, attendance was reduced to once per month in the end. I became more like a social worker to him out of pity for his plight. He had his own practice at one time but something happened that he wouldn't talk about and now he lives a solitary life and does chiropractic under the table to anyone he can find. On a few occasions, he called and asked for "an advance" on his next treatment because he didn't have any money.

"Your problem may be in the C vertebrae," he said, gently putting his warm fingers on my neck. "The back is very top-heavy. If you have something out of alignment above something else, it will constantly pull things below it out."

A lot was learned from him about the back. I listened carefully and asked a lot of questions. But my neurosurgeon said to let no one go near the neck. And I had deep resignation about him manipulating the cervical vertebrae, or neck vertebrae, which is what he meant when he said the C vertebrae.

"My neurosurgeon said expressly not let any chiropractor manipulate my neck," the information was relayed to him.

"Okay, okay," he said disappointedly. "No neck."

He would say this periodically for about the last year-and-a-half that I saw him. He had tried everything else and insisted that the neck was probably the problem. One winter day I began to cave out of the frustration in dealing with the pain.

"Look, I have a shunt with tubes that go through thought the neck. This, I believe, it is the primary concern for my neurosurgeon. If you take a shot at my neck you have to show that you will not damage the tube that runs down my neck or damage the shunt."

"Absolutely," he said instantly and delightedly.

"That's the beauty of the Gonstead approach. I am only going to target the specific vertebrae and there will be no violent twisting of your neck."

And with that, powerful desperation consented. This is how little I cared about life and how much the back pain tortured. There was absolutely no evidence that anything he did worked.

Why was this allowed? Desperation.

He began incorporating the manipulation of the neck into treatments. It was utterly useless like almost everything else he did. He was honest about not twisting the neck, however. He would angle it in a very precise way and give it the slightest turn, almost a flick. A very loud crack would sound that was much more startling than those in the back.

But it didn't help.

Then there was that November morning. It was a Saturday and it was extremely cold, below zero. There was ice everywhere and despite the weather, I drove to his mom's house. He gave our usual hour and half treatment. At the end of it, he went for the neck.

However, this crack was different. He manipulated, and the manipulation felt forced. I felt pain creep down it. When it was over, though, I could still move my neck fine and felt fine. I paid him and drove home.

The next morning, I could not move it to the right. This rigidity lasted over a week. It made work even harder and can still remember co-workers asking, "What's wrong with your neck?" I was terrified and panicked. Every second that was not spent at work, there were hot rice pads on or an electric heating pad on it. The texts sent read, “Since I saw you last, my neck can’t move. I’m terrified that last neck manipulation really hurt me. What should I do?”

I did not show anger. I also did not get a reply — at least at first. He waited a few days before texting back.

“Sorry to hear. It sounded like a good manipulation.”

And that was it. He did not offer to come in and get another manipulation to fix it. He did not offer some other kind of treatment to ease the pain. It was so disappointing and devastating. It felt like another betrayal.

I did not reply to him or ever see him again. He did not reach out, either. To this day — years later — it freezes up if I sleep on it incorrectly and it freezes up in the exact spot that he manipulated it incorrectly that day. Also, and more alarmingly, since then any CAT scan that is gotten reveals that the shunt tube was disconnected and no longer works. Another brain operation would have been necessary to fix the shunt. But since 2001, the meninges, which drain the fluid, must have cleaned themselves from the blood that was in them.

As Antaeus, I seemed to have finally met a barrier too big. After overcoming a traumatic brain injury, surviving lifelong OCD, and managing a daily battle with bipolar disorder, a mere back pain was the straw that broke the camel's back. On my list of "treatments tried," there are thirty-two different therapies or treatments for the back that were given a full therapeutic trial. Every one of them was either something that hurt me or an utter waste of time. Most were an utter waste of time.

For instance, "spinal decompression" was undergone. Twice per week for about two months I drove for forty-five minutes to get to the clinic and forty-five minutes to get back after work. A bunch of extremely superficial Tony Robbins types were the employees. They had the entire floor of the building and they all wore similar clothes and said similar things and quite frankly were a little bit creepy. They would strap my body into a machine and I was lying down. For fifteen minutes, the spine was pulled apart and held and then released. It did this in timed intervals. It felt very good and the idea was the disc that was out (if a disc was out) was sucked back into place by the pulling apart and returning motion that the machine performed.

"How often does this work?" I asked one of many overly optimistic drones who buzzed around the many clients getting this done.

"Ninety percent of the time," one of the drones said reflexively.

"That's been studied? And for what condition?"

"For all conditions," he said robotically. "And yes, we have performed studies. It works ninety percent of the time."

I probably should've walked out then and there. But desperation makes you do funny things. I really hoped that despite the false promising charlatans who ran the place, it worked at least five percent of the time. But it did not work. I just dropped about $400 in co-pays and gas.

I always went back to the medical profession despite their blindness. For someone who cannot get an MRI medicine is blind for back issues. Considering the stakes, it was conceivably suicide to get an MRI. If I died, it would destroy Mom and Dad, and that was too much to bear. It was the same sentiment that prevented literal suicide.

There was a doctor close to my apartment. I went to see him.

"There are a few ways to get an image of what we are dealing with or without an MRI." He said enthusiastically. "You can get a myelogram, for instance."

A myelogram is a procedure wherein the spine would be injected with a contrast dye and then I would be x-rayed. It would, theoretically, give a better picture of what was going on.

This doctor was seen back when the neurosurgeon who saved my life was still alive. I consulted my neurosurgeon regarding the procedure.

"A doctor in New York who I am seeing wants me to get a myelogram," I said nervously to Dr. Sedor's secretary. "I gave him Dr. Sedor's number so they can talk about whether it is safe."

Dr. Sedor called back personally. "Under no circumstances can you get that myelogram," he said sternly. "You don't need one and it could hurt you."

I disappointedly agreed and listened to whatever

he said. Upon returning to the doctor, I will never forget what happened.

"I can't see you anymore," he said as he stood in his small, new age sort of office that was set up very neatly. It was shocking. "Your neurosurgeon called. He feels, uhh, very strongly about you not getting a myelogram. He actually called on the phone and evidently feels very strongly about you. I am really not comfortable seeing you as a patient anymore."

Another option was out. But there was an even stronger love and admiration for who would be my late neurosurgeon within the year.

At this point, thirty-two examinations, treatments, or therapies were undergone. And after all that, I was no further along figuring out or having a specific diagnosis for my back. It was, like everything else in this life, another waking nightmare. There is great pain and great irony in the fact that a device used to save this life from one nightmare is the same device that prohibits finding out about or treating another nightmare is the definition of Albert Camus' absurdity.

Some strides were made on their own. Each day, I focus on writing at the desk for five, ten, fifteen, and eventually twenty minutes. I retrained my body to gradually be able to write at a desk rather than writing with the journal on top of my lap while I sat on the couch. Slowly, but surely, writing at the desk was possible again and I was so grateful to be able to do so. This took about two years of writing on the couch in a seated position before it was possible.

The same technique did not work with typing, or anything else for that matter. Everything else got better incrementally but then the progress reached its peak and the pain continued on.

And so my back unexpectedly joined OCD, bipolar disorder, and traumatic brain injury as the four giants that would knock me to the ground each and every day. I used the techniques described earlier, such as the low keyboard drawer, lots of breaks, never standing for long, and many others to circumvent the pain or to better endure it.

This went on for about four years and all hope was lost in curing the pain and I thought about quitting many times. The problem was I could not find even the possibility of another job that I could do around it. What social work job does not require standing or typing, is not too social, would accept not leaving your office for at least half the year, and that also would allow many breaks to go to the bathroom or perform any other rituals that OCD demanded? What I had was, probably, the best of all possible worlds. So the desperate search for some kind of a solution went on.

There were no illusions about the physical pain. Whatever was wrong would have to be lived with long term. I searched and searched for a voice activated software program that typed so the back didn't have to take the brutal beating it did daily.

And it was found. A software program called Nuance's Dragon NaturallySpeaking saved the job and improved employment immensely. It was very much doubted that it would work at first. The software was fully researched and purchased and its installation was allowed at the agency I worked. It worked almost perfectly initially and has only gotten better since then. It is used every day and I've not typed many keys since. I could not be more grateful for it and it truly has saved a lot of anguish.

Therefore, in the end, back pain was not defeated. It has not changed. To this day, I cannot stand for more than a few minutes without leg numbness. Typing remains difficult. And there is still no definitive answer of what is wrong or hope of it being known in the future.

However, it was endured and transcended. It has thrown me to the ground for a total of thirteen years to this point. It shows no indication that it will relent. The problem is not solved. With the voice software, however, it was totally circumvented. Amidst the pain of almost any giant, there is a way – a method – a trick – to work around its nightmare. Every giant, like David's Goliath, contains a weakness. Finding it is, admittedly, an excruciating endeavor. But it can be done.

Back pain has made me stronger. First, it has done a lot to improve the ability to endure recurrent pain. Expecting each day to hurt makes you tougher. Strength has also come mentally from enduring it. A great deal of personal research has given adequate knowledge of the back and how it works and that gives strength for how to contend with its pain.

It also spurred a lot of creative problem solving. There was an endless amount of positions and techniques that had to be devised in order to work around it.

As always, lots of help was given along the way. But it was personal ingenuity that went the furthest toward finding ways around it. Back pain, therefore, like traumatic brain injury, like OCD, and like bipolar disorder watches and waits for more opportunities to knock me down on a daily basis. Using thought to find ways around it has made all the difference.

V

ANTAEUS AT COLLEGE

EVERYTHING ACHIEVED COMES AT a price. That price can take many forms. But as long as you can use your skills and strengths to pay that price you will always be empowered to continue to achieve your goals.

Getting a bachelor's degree was really hard. It was pre-Lithium. Four different schools were attended. It took seven years to get a four year degree. Footsteps were counted to every class — or else. Repeating everything said in class was mandatory. Memory was so atrocious. It was so bad that the only way to survive was to write a short summary in every single paragraph of every single book read so that it could be recalled. It was painstaking and took many hours each night. All of life, from waking until sleep, was school and mental illness.

Then there was bipolar disorder. This was the principal reason it took seven years to get a degree.

"I'm sorry, but I need to take off next semester," were

the fearful words I uttered to my academic advisor. There was such shame in saying it. But in the end it was easier to do that than to go to class afraid of all the people in it. In some classes, sweat poured profusely on the way to class due to the social anxiety. Imagining that it was only the professor and I in the room sometimes helped. This is what gave me the courage to talk. It was, in a way, just us. No one else spoke to me and I talked to no one else. Sometimes I sensed resentment from my peers because class was made longer by asking a lot of questions. I felt like a pariah and while it was never said directly to me, I'd catch classmates shrug once in a while when asking question after question because it prolonged the class.

Attending college was like a dark and endless march without the electric current. Cognition became impossible and it was only support from Mom that enabled survival.

"Did you understand that, honey?" She said in a tone that was kind and empathetic and caring.

"Yes." This was a lie. And Mom knew it was. There was too much confusion throughout the depressions — and she knew when it was being understood or not. In the glorious manias, techniques were constantly being developed to cope, but the depressions always stomped out any hope that those techniques were viable. It was literally as if a different body was switched out from underneath me.

"Okay, well here's what it said," Mom said and then summarized it in a line. It was short, quick synopses that made it through the fog and memory problems that were omnipresent.

It was all very grueling. It was during this period that, out of frustration, I would occasionally hit myself with utter fury and rage. The traumatic brain injury teamed up with the OCD and the bipolar disorder and made it so that there was little comprehension of what was being read, or, eliminated the memory of what was read. It was Kafkaesque.

After attending class, the assignments would be a mystery. The books seemed like they were written by the teacher in Charlie Brown.

"I — am — useless — I — can't — remember — or — understand — anything — I — am — going — to — live — in — a — cardboard — box."

This was said to Mom regularly. Each dash represents a punch to my body. Anything that destroyed this torture chamber — this body — was pleasant no matter how much pain it caused.

Every single day was a struggle. It was during this period that the shotgun was purchased with Dad's help and was consigned to the ultimate end of suicide.

But there were just enough manias and help from Mom to barely survive. All of the very hard work paid off but there were no extracurricular activities or friends — just studying. The degree received from King's College says *summa cum laude* — the highest honor in an undergraduate degree due to a perfect GPA — 4.0. There was no social life and every day was incredibly hard work performed amidst a haze of disabling problems. Exactly one party was attended through all of college, through one friend I met and spoke to once every few months. But it got accomplished. The degree was gained despite all of the disabilities.

In addition, all the awards given out by the English faculty were given to me. The professors gave both of the awards for outstanding achievement, a tremendous feat that I never saw coming. I truly cherish the awards today. However, social anxiety prevented attendance to graduation. The depression was all-consuming.

None of these disabling conditions could have been overcome without tremendous help. Already noted was the immense support of Mom, who helped with everything. But she was not all. Professors, for instance, were very compassionate when I occasionally broke down and approached them.

"I didn't understand anything on that test," was said to a history professor just after the test was finished. "It's this depression … I am so sorry … There is proof that I'm not making this up … medical proof."

It was very humbling. It was said in his office just after the test.

"Well, let's find out how you did," the professor said with a smile. "You do excellent work, Kurt." He took the test as we stood in his classroom after everyone had left.

Few classes were missed in college, but when they were, the professors understood. The classes where Dr.

Jekyll — the mania — took over were filled with constant participation. I went on and on and on. The classes where Mr. Hyde — the depression — was present were filled with an intense anxiety and desire for invisibility and the chair I sat in was positioned as far back in the room as possible. The professors never pushed too far. They were great.

Then there was the Office of Vocational Rehabilitation. There was a wonderful counselor from there who visited. She helped to make it affordable by giving a small subsidy each semester of undergraduate school.

SSI also helped immensely. The money from SSI enabled some pocket cash. Part-time work along with school would have been simply overwhelming. Most of those years, going to full-time school was a Herculean task that was wildly overwhelming. Part-time college was often all that was manageable. Part-time work couldn't possibly be handled on top of it. SSI was a godsend and it enabled education and success to occur.

It was around this time that religion also played a major aid as well. Christianity always was a motivator. Whether through OCD fears of the afterlife or through the teachings and philosophy of brotherhood and love, it always motivated. It made meaning because the teachings gave meaning and gave direction — a purpose.

There was tremendous help. And it could not have been done without that help. It took tremendous personal strength and a humble willingness to fail much more often than succeed.

Many similar struggles were endured in the gaining of a master's degree. It was done the same way and the same formula was used. The help and the resources in the environment were assessed and utilized in the same way. The effort was made to continually to get up off the ground each time I was forced to it. It was a struggle that seemed utterly insurmountable most times. It was like the feeling of reading a book and being almost sure of what was going to happen but hoping it somehow comes out differently.

My biggest external asset in the battle against my ailments was the belonging and guidance received from my support network.

Mom deserves to be in some kind of Mother Hall of Fame for her selfless dedication. The existence of a support network — whatever form that may take — can be one of the best assets you have in the dubious battle against your problems. Whether you do or not, however, everyone has resources around them that they can use to overcome or ease their pain. It is nice to think that everyone has other human beings around them who can be relied on and who can care for them. But we know that is not true. We can, however, say that good people are out there and some people will care.

Finding them is a behemoth task because they are very, very rare. Words cannot express how helpful it is to have not just someone who listens but who also loves you. Mom's and later Tanya's love made all the difference in empowering forward movement and to keep getting up off the ground.

After my undergraduate degree, the new setting from graduate school and the new people in Binghamton did not help my mental health. They provided more alienation and more isolation.

These are the circumstances under which I began studying for the master's degree. Coping mechanisms were learned very fast for fear of failure. The bulk of social work classes consisted of group work. This means that students are broken down into small groups to discuss and solve a problem together. Throughout many classes during the master's degree — as well as bachelor's degree — cognition was clouded by a remarkable mental fog. However, the material was read so thoroughly before class (every word of it) and so many notes were taken in the margins that despite the fog, enough information got in. This gave a great advantage in the groups and in class in general. A major advantage was caring so much and another was OCD's perfectionism because it prohibited failure. A tremendous amount of time was put into learning and relearning the material.

"They are looking for the strengths perspective," I said in a moment of courage in the groups. Classmates were all much better at talking in the group and sharing their experiences in social work and so on and so forth. Knowledge of the book was my major strength.

If there were four people in a group, one was always assigned the role of scribe. Being too foggy and too nervous to remember everything that was being said, this role was purposely avoided. Another role, however, was speaker. This was a socially anxious torture and it was avoided at all costs. So, learning to speak in a small group was a lesser evil than having to speak in large groups. Nervousness was omnipresent, hands were always were coated with nervous sweat, and the intense anxiety created forgetfulness of half of what I read, which, again, was the only real strength in the group.

Years of going through this made a dent in the social anxiety through classical conditioning. The undergraduate degree contained almost no groups at all. The graduate degree served as classical conditioning to learn how to function in a group. It became clear that even when I didn't know every answer, nobody laughed. To be honest, nobody cared. And it became easier to fail.

Throughout the course of the master's degree, presentations were also done often. And then there was the role-playing. Role-playing was bearable in the hypomanias. But during the downs, they were excruciating. OCD, as always, demanded absolute perfection. Perfection was always fallen short of.

And that was the key to survival. Learning to fail. I repeated to myself John Steinbeck's statement, "And now that you don't have to be perfect, you can be good," to be a reminder of what was important: being good, not being perfect.

Learning the best way to overcome a fear is to face it and even fail at it was very therapeutic. Learning that it was not nearly as horrible to fail was perceived as liberating. It was nothing like the true terrors, like severe and suicidal depression or the endless web of imprisonment that is OCD. Facing fears became the defense. Never was a fear completely destroyed. But each one was faced. Music was the source of great comfort during my adolescent years and to this day, I have found no music is better than that of The Doors. Their lead singer, Jim Morrison, wrote,

> *Expose yourself to your deepest fear; after that, fear has no power, and the fear of freedom shrinks and vanishes. You are free.*

This was positively true in the case of my fears. Each one was faced and each one terrorized but each one taught me it was not the end of the world to fail. In fact, there was strength in failure. And gradually, the fear of failing lost its power. This freedom to continue to fail due to those giants was liberating. The freedom to fail also gave the strength to focus on solutions rather than always focusing on pride and vanity. In short, failing can be liberating and can free us so that we can learn to overcome.

Therefore, it became clear that failing was nothing like the true terrors – like severe depression or the endless web of incarceration that is obsessive compulsive disorder. Facing fears became my defense and strategy. Failing was the game plan. No fear was destroyed. But each and every one was faced.

"Next semester's schedule is too impossible. This is too much," I would say to one of the directors at the graduate college. He was extremely compassionate.

"Why don't we try an online elective?" he asked.

"Okay, but what about the other classes?"

He sat thoughtfully. "Well, now that it is known that you have these issues, we have some options. I will be sensitive to them in class. The other professors here will understand and be sensitive to your mental health concerns if you tell them, too. But that is your choice."

After that meeting, more professors were told about the mental health issues. I asked them merely to be cognizant that they exist, that they were out in the open. It helped a great deal psychologically to know that they knew about bipolar and the TBI. The OCD could be hidden. It was the depressions and the memory that had no defense.

Few friends were made in graduate school just as few friends were made everywhere I've been. This, as always, exacerbated all issues. Solitude was like gasoline on the fire of pain and made overcoming these giants harder. The fact is that I only ever really had Mom, Angelo, and later, Tanya, and this made it incredibly solitary most of the time after leaving Pennsylvania.

I journaled constantly. Journaling, along with the characters in my stories, were, in their own ways, like other friends. Writing very much dulled the pain of poor socialization.

Loneliness made it so that the world was essentially just my OCD, bipolar, back pain, and TBI. They became my identity after a while. Each day, every day, they were all there was. The same techniques were used as in undergraduate school to work. However, when OCD's commands are the only things you ever "hear" and depression's lethargic, confused, numbness is all you ever feel, there routinely comes a tipping point. There was no one there for consistent comfort and I wrestled a great with these enemies in my mind. I began to experiment with alcohol despite all the warnings against it. I was deceived into thinking that the neurosurgeon never forbade me from drinking and that there was no scientific reason that drinking was prohibited. I didn't want to believe this former escape was gone.

So, drinking began. I loved it. Alcohol enabled temporary departure from the nightmare. More specifically, alcohol made it so there was no care about the many problems that plagued consciousness.

Dad was a severe alcoholic. That's often an inherited gene. So before long, seven to ten shots of drinking per night became normal. The drinks were scientifically managed and titrated up slowly to see how it would affect my brain. Every night one more shot would be had and a record of its affects were recorded the following day. For a short time, it was as if an old ally returned in the fight for my life.

That is, until research on the cerebellum began. Alcohol directly affects and destroys the cerebellum in everyone. Many cases of severe alcoholics losing their ability to walk and to balance over time due to alcohol's incredible destruction can be found in the literature. It is completely unknown what alcohol would do to a person with one side of his cerebellum removed.

This was horrifying and half of the appeal of alcohol was ripped away and shrouded by a profound fear. Every time a step was taken, the fear that it would be the last step taken haunted every minute of every day. The problem was despite this new horror and fear, drinking continued anyway because the fear was still outweighed by having to face each day with the four-headed monster of bipolar depression, OCD, back pain, and TBI.

The neurosurgeon was consulted about the decision to drink nightly.

"You are drinking?" he asked after he was told about using alcohol as a coping mechanism.

"Yes." And as it was said, his face change entirely. He looked devastated at this response. It was very powerful. It was absolutely crushing that I ever did anything to hurt the doctor who did so much.

"How much?"

"Between seven and ten shots daily." This was, at that time, underestimating the amount due to his upset look.

I will never forget how large his eyes opened. He seemed to be expecting only very little, like one or two at dinner or something minimal like that. He looked stunned and almost like he was betrayed.

Dr. Sedor had a female assistant who was at the visit. She was in the room and told a story about it. She was very pretty and she had a heavy German accent.

"You are taking a horrible chance when you drink," she interjected. "We have had many patients who have had brain injuries nowhere near as severe as yours. Some of those patients drank. It never ends up well. For instance, we had one gentleman who started drinking heavily like you are and one morning he woke up and could no longer remember anything. His short-term memory vanished. He could remember who he was and where he came from and his past but could remember nothing current."

An avalanche of fear descended into me. "I didn't know that was possible."

"Well, it is," she said after her cautionary tale. "There are many other examples as well," she said and just after that her phone went off. She excused herself and left the room.

The doctor who saved my life looked sternly at me.

"Kurt, you are playing roulette with your brain. You have a very unique brain injury and there is no study to cite or knowledge to give of what will happen if you continue drinking. What can be said is that it will be bad — very bad. You are taking a horrible chance with your brain every time you take a drink."

This all came very fast and was very frightening. His care was touching and it was obviously very important to him that more damage was not done by the substance that seemed to provide so much relief.

"Okay, Dr. Sedor." He was sitting directly across from my chair. "However, alcohol provides the single best release for the pain of these depressions. Is there any amount of alcohol that is safe? Can two or three shots each night be drunk just to feel a little relief?"

There was no pause before the response. "No one can say exactly what will happen to you if you continue to drink any amount. I'll say it again. You have a very unique brain injury, Kurt, and there are no studies done on it and little is known about people who don't have a large part of their cerebellum. So neither I nor any other doctor cannot tell you what will happen if you drink at all.

"What can be said is that no amount of alcohol is safe for you. And if your brain does not handle it well, no one could say just how terrible it will be for you. What can be said is that it will most likely affect your coordination and ability to walk. Your memory is also at high risk. However, there are many other horrible things that can happen from your drinking alcohol. No amount is safe."

Until he died, Dr. Sedor never forgot to ask if I was still drinking in every single appointment after that one. He had a million patients but he always remembered this and everything that happened to me. The importance of not drinking alcohol was obvious.

Nevertheless, alcohol brought what was craved. The obsessive thoughts and fear of future horrors were drowned out and all that mattered was the present and getting relief. In addition, alcohol helped socialization. For a few months after speaking to Dr. Sedor, not a drop was touched. But the sadness crept back in. And then came an offer from a classmate,

"Hey Kurt, you want to go to the bar for a few drinks

after class?" the classmate asked. This marked the second time in my life that a classmate had offered to go somewhere. There was immense pressure to accept the invitation despite the fact that it was around alcohol. How could you turn it down? The intention was to only have one drink. However, it was wonderful to be out of the tiny room I rented. So, the classmate and I went and enjoyed good conversation and, inevitably, drinking occurred. It was so nice and intellectual and pleasant and before long he became a "drinking buddy." It was so disappointing that this was the only way socialization could occur.

After the brain injury, it still took around six years to completely cut alcohol out entirely. The first rule was to drink only when I was out — for socialization purposes. Then when that didn't work, the second rule became trying to drink only at home. Then when that didn't work, I imposed a very specific limit on the amount of drinks that could be had, home or out. Another rule that was made was going to the bar with a limited amount of ways to pay to limit consumption. But this failed miserably, too. I am just so grateful that somehow worse damage was never done. I thank God each and every day that He allowed this body to forgive me for the worst decision ever made – to continue drinking. It was a worse decision than all the others.

The master's degree was received in 2013. Those years were filled with many days of personal agony. It took a full six years since it was started to achieve that meaningful goal. Each day I was truly Antaeus and each day I got up a little stronger and a little more hateful of this world. But each day I got up. In 2019, I attained social work licensure through New York State.

The suffering was tremendous. But the degree was achieved and licensure was received. All was worked around and both were gotten. And now, with the degree and the license, it was time to make meaning of my life. And I fervently believed that that meaning could enable the endurance of all those disabilities. That was the thesis when leaving Pennsylvania and it was the thesis in New York and with the social work degree.

Making the world a little bit less of a nightmare was meaningful and it redirected the focus away from suffering. Meaning and purpose enabled me to transcend and deemphasize being thrown to the ground over and over again.

And above all, a moral life was being lived.

This was hope for the future.

VI

ANTAEUS AT WORK

MY FUTURE BEGAN WITH working. Working started shortly after meeting Angelo in graduate school. Employment added to school began in 2008. It was incredibly difficult and frightening but it was actually less difficult than sitting at home and enduring the thoughts. Pushing myself became constant and seldom was a workday missed. Work became a welcome keystone of life.

In the chapter on working around back pain, I detailed how this was accomplished at the job. As noted, the process was very brutal and it took time and my compassionate supervisor gave me the creative leeway that was necessary to work around the disability.

I did not, however, detail how I worked around OCD, the bipolar disorder, and the traumatic brain injury. There can be a great deal of overwhelming and unseen challenges if you are going to transcend and overcome your problems. These challenges often go beyond finding ways to counteract and mitigate the problem itself. This is to say that many unexpected challenges often arise once you are enveloped by the social world and other worlds that are often included in work. This chapter details some of the difficulties I experienced and overcame in order to engage in the meaningful activity that work can provide.

My OCD always went, as far as I know, undetected by coworkers. Introversion and isolation made it relatively easy to shield it from coworkers, clients, etc. Only the extremely dry skin and cracks on my hands could give it away.

I did, however, write a company newsletter as an intern and did disclose many issues I suffered in it. Only one or two co-workers ever really made a comment. Basically, OCD did not hurt employment from a social standpoint whatsoever.

What OCD did affect, however, is every day at work. It wrapped its tentacles around everything. Every report or progress note had to be in a certain order and checked and rechecked and rechecked and rechecked.

When leaving the agency at night, OCD "said" that if everything is not perfectly arranged and in perfect order and symmetrical, something horrible will happen. It took extra time to leave each night — after clocking out. Checking and rechecking the locks everywhere was a "necessity" because it is certain that someone will break in. Just imagine your paranoia about feeling the people in the offices nearby "knowing" that you are "crazy" because they saw you leave and come back over and over until everything was "right."

Every day, new obsessions kept bobbing to the surface of consciousness. Every day, I kept facing them and knocking them down one after the other. It was an endless battle then and it is now, too. I find it remarkable that every phase, from checking to repeating, from hoarding to pure obsession, to an endless desire for everything to be perfectly and unendingly symmetrical, still remain. They are all very weakened by my constant assaults, but they all remain.

"Kurt, I'm not a bit worried about your books," Angelo always said, referring to the books kept for the program at work. This involves three-ring binders for every client full of eight sections of information that was collected on each client. There was a second set of binders that accounted for all of the finances that were sent out to the state showing what was spent and all of the statistics the state asked me to report. "There is no doubt that your OCD has them in perfect shape," he always said with a smile. But the point was true. He never worried about my records or bookkeeping at all. There has been no time in the thirteen years I worked at that agency that the books have not been meticulously kept and in perfect order.

Most maladies inflicted upon us are not all bad. There are small gifts intertwined with virtually any horrible condition. Being extremely neat and organized is one such way to become visibly stronger through the adversity of OCD. Supervisors and others find what I do at work to be exact and orderly and on time. It is. And OCD is owed in large part for that.

However, despite these gifts, OCD makes your life

very, very difficult as should be evident. However, the struggle is an internal one. Externally, OCD can help make your work precise and exact and very reliable.

"Kurt," Angelo said, "take a break and come to lunch."

Oftentimes I'd decline this offer. This was often because of social anxiety or the obsessive need to keep rechecking something or make sure something is perfect. Sometimes Angelo saw this.

"It's right! It's right!" he exclaimed in reply.

But there's never certainty that is right. That is the issue. OCD is the mental illness of uncertainty. There's never really certainty in anything. In high school, I began referring to OCD as a disorder with philosophical basis that is a Cartesian in nature. All that is clear is that I think, therefore I am. Everything else has to be checked over and over to make certain.

Because of the brain injury and the memory damage, OCD always makes compelling arguments to check everything one more time. This is why doubting/checking is probably the most prominent obsession since the brain injury at work. It forced checking and rechecking by using the brain injury as evidence of why checking needs to be done again.

"How is your OCD, Kurt?" Mom would ask me.

"It is like a large, very pesky fly constantly in my face."

That is true, but it is really far more debilitating than that. There is a certain comfort in convincing yourself that you will never end up with disabling OCD like so many others. But it is a false comfort. This chapter is being written with several deep and red cracks in my hands from all of the washing done every day. I bleed from them and every night before going to bed Band-Aids have to be put around the cuts and moisturizer is put on the Band-Aids when things are particularly painful. If OCD was obeyed to the full extent, there is no doubt that my OCD would be disabling.

The bipolar disorder, if left untreated, would cause suicide. If that trigger could not be pulled, the only other option would be living under a bridge or on the streets. The depressions come with such terror and with such vehemence that it is like trying to resist someone who is drowning you — for months. It is impossible. Something would have broken within a year or two if Lithium was not properly prescribed to me.

Bipolar disorder was able to be worked around while in college. This was only possible because college was an extremely solitary affair. There were no social heirs put on whatsoever. Still, going to college was perfectly brutal nonetheless because of bipolar disorder. College life was spent trying to figure out ways to circumvent it and not let it destroy me.

Nevertheless, like OCD, I was always able to barely find a way to retain employment around bipolar disorder. The type of bipolar disorder that I experienced enabled me to have very small windows of time wherein I was exceptionally productive. In these periods of time, I was better than just functional. These hypomanias are undoubtedly the bright side of bipolar and for a short time, brilliant work can be done and that work can sometimes make up for the dormant periods. In the depressions, there is nothing to do but utilize whatever strengths you have to find a way to function and to communicate with those around you.

One of the most severe issues with bipolar disorder from a work perspective is the social realm. Socialization often proves to be remarkably arduous and painful for anyone with bipolar disorder. Therefore, working in a halfway house with fourteen other individuals around all the time — almost all of whom had legal histories and were not wildly friendly — was really difficult.

What nearly broke me, though, was the callousness of co-workers at work.

In a lucid mania, I closed the office door one day at the halfway house. It was warm and stuffy in the small room but everyone was in good spirits and it was a good time to do what needed to be done. The focus of my discourse were two women who worked together at the halfway house.

"One day, not too long from now, I am going to go upstairs into my office and am not going to come back out. This is due to a very severe mental illness. You are my friends now. In the last five months, we've gotten to know each other and I have come to think of you as real friends. When this happens, and it will, I need you to not let me stay up there. I need you both to help through the downs. Because a down is coming soon and it cannot be escaped."

"Oh, yes," the two women nodded. Both agreed readily and both acted very helpful in all ways. "No problem, Kurt. We'll be there for you."

However, when the time came, neither of them helped. Instead of help, they hindered. They would, for instance, engage in all kinds of social gatherings with both the clients and other coworkers downstairs but would make sure not to extend an invitation to these gatherings. Even worse, I was made to feel like an outsider whenever around them and often times when walking into the room they were in, they stopped talking. They were sure to include the other halfway house workers in all of the parties and meetings but never told me. They isolated me in a way that seemed very purposeful and very malicious. Those two women treated me poorly and after a while it was obvious that they just wanted me out of the job. Needless to say, they furthered my distrust and alienation and skepticism of others.

The relationship with them at work was just another form of being knocked to the ground yet again. This time, it was being knocked down by environmental forces rather than biological ones. After that, I didn't really speak to anyone but the residents in the program and Angelo. Mom continued to provide the only social warmth in brief phone calls during the day.

Those two women made working in the halfway house much harder and infinitely worse than it had to be and many of us have coworkers like this and they detract from everything in our work world. You may be familiar with this kind of social ostracism and cruelty as it often occurs to individuals who are down, have problems, and feel alienated. Throughout those four years, until Tanya came along, there was no one who I completely trusted or talked to at work.

But it was accomplished. I endured it, learned from it, and became stronger from it as from everything else. You find ways to become stronger. With the new counselors who came into the house, every attempt was made to connect and bond with them before the two women downstairs could get to them.

One of those counselors was Tanya. For those three or four months of the year that hypomania animated me, allies were forged with wherever possible.

I found ways through my weaknesses and you can find ways through your weaknesses, too. That is the thesis of this book. Working around disabilities is not happy or pleasurable. But you can find ways to subvert at least some of your issues. You can find ways to survive. But every depressive day can be an immeasurably large, a David versus Goliath, battle even with these ways.

Each day before work I would kneel before the Bible and just pray ardently that the torture be manageable throughout the day and that the strength could be summoned to endure it.

A new office was eventually, after many years, given to me at that job and it was finally away from those women. This was wonderful. It made work a lot easier.

But still, every meeting at the agency was social horror in the depressions. All of the meetings that could be hidden from were and the ones that were unavoidable were spent in utter silence. Talking at meetings was terrifying throughout all of the downs. Trying to avoid confrontation at all costs was very important in the depressions. Everything was slow and confusing and intimidating. Many meetings were left not knowing what was said or what went on. Memory seemed absent. Periods of the day were usually spent looking for where I parked my car because there was no recollection as to where it was parked.

Was there any relief each day when severely depressed? Yes. There was an hour lunch every day. A sandwich was purchased at a local deli and then it was off to a local park. The car was parked in front of a pond with beautiful high trees swaying back and forth and all around in the cool winds of upstate New York. Birds chirped all around as the food was eaten and the depression always made the food uninteresting and taste poorly and it would have to be forced down.

During the lunches that were eaten depressed, I just stared forward. The pond looked so tranquil but the thoughts — the tortured and obsessed thoughts — were very much a foil to the pond. The thoughts were awful and when your thoughts are awful, everything is.

But paradoxically it was wonderful, too, because I wasn't "there." There was no obligation to pay attention or concentrate or actively force functioning. Think mindfulness. It was excruciating to constantly be forcing yourself to move and to think and to concentrate when you don't have any will or desire or energy to do so. The seat was reclined as far back as it could go in the car and that aching back was rested — the aching back that was screaming in pain by noon each day from typing.

But again, a way was and is always found. The therapist argued that lunch was one of those "simple pleasures" that should be savored. This sentiment really helped. Sitting alone and eating lunch and calling Mom were always the best part of the day. Nature was healing in the same way it was healing for great writers such as Shelley, Keats, Coleridge, Emerson, and Thoreau.

Little crutches like this were created everywhere and you can make these, too. The concept of "simple pleasures" aids you when you are suffering a great deal. For instance, from 2001, when the head injury occurred to 2013, when we got married, I smoked three cigarettes per day. If truth is being told, four were smoked many of those days because insomnia always necessitates another. At four in the morning it was always time for another "simple pleasure."

Cigarettes are disgusting and terrible. There are

no real redeeming qualities of them. However, smoking became a perceived means to an end after the brain injury. There were myriad of reasons why. They served as a very minor psycho stimulant and improved memory very slightly, for instance. This reasoning was self-justification. Another reason cigarettes were so appealing then was they tapped into my *Thanatos*, what Freud called the death drive. I figured that God may not view smoking as direct suicide because it is done over decades. It was also reasoned that one artery was cut in my brain – the left vertebral artery. This meant that only three major general arteries were left that fed the brain. If a stroke could occur in another artery, the burden of this life was definitely over.

This was the thought process every day. However, on the other side of that thought process was the possibility of another survived stroke. Then, I'd even be worse off than ever. To paraphrase Candide's *Pangloss*: This was the worst of all possible worlds. So, "hedging my bets," I decided to keep the pleasure of smoking while only taking a minimal risk of having a stroke. Three cigarettes per day were smoked very rigidly. All of them were smoked at night and those little death sticks were looked forward to with all the excitement that a puppy looks forward to a treat.

Many simple pleasures like this and a multitude of other ways to work around each and every nightmare that bipolar disorder created were tremendous assets in sustaining employment. It is also very important to note that all the while I had a boss who was one of my few friends and checked on me often to see how I was doing. This, along with Mom and Tanya, made an enormous difference.

One extremely important issue in terms of employment with bipolar disorder was the previously mentioned cognitive fog. Each day of the depressions, all day, a deep fog surrounded all thought. This mental fog made accessing information extremely difficult or impossible at times. Perpetual confusion ensued. Even if something was studied intensely, when it came time to access it, the fog consumed all.

We all have a cognitive fog at some point in our lives and that fog can be caused by many things. It is universal. I meticulously charted and found and developed a few techniques to weather it through these many periods of dense fog. Silence, for instance, was a major weapon... because I knew no one else knew the fog was there and therefore could hide in silence.

The second method was self-titled, "learning the essence." For instance, rather than get bogged down in remembering the details of Paul Revere and Lexington and Concord, "learning the essence" was knowing that the Revolutionary War was fought because America was tired of being ruled unfairly by England. The details after that didn't matter because they would be forgotten anyway. It was a major subjective victory if the essence of what someone said could be learned amidst the fog.

I use the metaphor of a fog for its accuracy. Imagine trying to navigate the world with a dense, white, early morning fog around you. You cannot access the sight you need to navigate the world properly. You just had to "learn the essence" of what was in front of you. Then, you just stayed quiet. The endless barrage of hideous thoughts and obsessions that came with the depressions was too encompassing for you to bother with the outside world. So silence came naturally. This technique was used extensively for over fifteen years before lithium lifted the fog that descended.

While bipolar disorder set an Odyssey-esque barrage of obstacles to navigate through school and employment, the traumatic brain injury had its own Scylla and Charybdis that was long-lasting and torturous throughout both work and school. The traumatic brain injury, as previously mentioned, principally tortured primarily through memory problems.

"And what happens to the referral after it goes in?" I asked Angelo.

He smiled. "It goes to the committee who votes on it. Then the person gets admitted."

This was during the six month internship done prior to getting employed. He, the head of all residential programs in the agency, took me, nobody, under his wing. He took me around with him and was his shadow often times.

"And what happens to the referral after it goes in?"

He smiled again and answered just as sincerely. "It goes to the committee who votes on it. Then the person gets admitted."

This was constantly done in the beginning with him. That is, the same question was asked over and over. There was no recollection that it was asked. He was extremely empathetic to the issues and smiled and answered the question each time as if it were the first time it was asked.

The only way it was known that the same question was being asked is because there was always a little notebook in my pocket. The lines of the pages were filled with "must remember things." This was a major tool around memory issues. In it was written,

"Referrals go to committee for admission."

Then a couple of lines or pages later it would read,

"Referrals — committee — admission."

It was very embarrassing. Once the redundancy was realized, gratitude was expressed to him for his patience. Then, after a day or two, I asked him again.

The greatest method of working around the memory problems of the traumatic brain injury will always be humility. But as with OCD and bipolar disorder, this and the other methods can only cover up or 'fake' so much. Memory was the major work hurdle that remained after my TBI. Walking and talking and all the other physical problems were relearned by this point. But memory was remarkably difficult to either hide or cover over.

"I already told you that!" was a common exclamatory remark from many people. So, I learned not to talk.

Memory issues were often met with hostility from people who are too busy to repeat themselves. But it was hard to navigate the social world without asking these people.

So in lieu of asking, I eventually became an expert at reading facial expressions and got answers in different ways. For instance, waiting for other people to ask the same question was a common technique. Another technique was studying the eyes of people when asking them questions. Learning when to proceed and when to back off was an acquired skill.

I used to almost fill one of those little notebooks per day with memory prompts. The notebooks trained my mind and I need to fill them less and less as my memory got stronger and stronger at work.

It was through this notebook and through very careful and metered organization that memory issues were managed. For instance, on the twenty-fifth day every month, the reports to the state agency were sent in. The only exception to this rule was when the 25th is a holiday or weekend. In this case, and regularly, there were a series of alarms that go off on the 23th or 24th or whatever weekday fell before the 25th reminding that the report is due to compensate for its falling on a weekend. Even after over a decade of doing it, those alarms were absolutely vital for the reports to be remembered.

Another technique for memory at work was organization. If items are put into one pile, it meant they had to be done. If they were in another pile, they didn't. This categorization — this taxonomy — is the keystone of so many of the memory aids. There is a place for absolutely everything. OCD found a place for anything and everything in my world. This is how OCD helps the bipolar disorder and the memory problems.

Careful and methodical note-taking and categorization systems are how work and school were navigated with such a battered and beaten memory. However, these techniques also had the added benefit of making memory much stronger. Today, due in large part to these exhaustive note-taking and categorization techniques, my memory is no longer terrible, it is very much a working memory. All these techniques serve as ongoing physical and cognitive therapy and strengthen memory the way a muscle is strengthened. Believe it or not, no one would ever know that I had a TBI unless it was said to them. Even neurosurgeons have made that comment. And it is very pleasurable to be able to walk into anywhere and not have to be burdened by the overwhelming stigma that any person with a brain injury, mental health condition, physical disability, etc. endures each and every day.

Despite what your culture tells you, appearance isn't everything. Society generally looks at you and says that if you don't look sick, you are not sick. But someone appearing healthy doesn't necessitate that health should be assumed. Appearances lie. And silence cannot be used as a way to "hide" it all the time. The only solutions to this are education and acceptance. And one day perhaps we can use understanding rather than appearance as our gauges for health as a society. It would make all the difference to the many of us who suffer in silence day after day.

At least once per week there is a situation wherein I have no memory of what was said in a past conversation. At least several times per week, you might see me wandering a parking lot looking for where the car is parked after coming out of a store. To these situations and a hundred other situations when the needed information is just not accessible, the humble and humorous response in the traumatic brain injury chapter is used. I turn to any company who is near or say to myself,

"Have I told you about my condition?"

This does two things. First, it's humbling and second, it acknowledges — and does not hide — that a problem exists. It's hiding it that creates anxiety. This comment makes any company laugh if he or she has seen and remembers the movie the line came from. And if they have not, then it makes for a fun and humbling conversation. This is the response to the issue of my memory since I can remember (I would give a date, but have I told you about my condition?).

Between humility and note taking and categorization, I can work around the TBI. It continues to affect me and always will but I will continue to work around its every limitation. The point is that finding a personal way to work around it using my strengths while being compassionate made work possible. If you use your strengths to find the way that works for you, I am confident that you'll climb new vistas of accomplishment too.

Despite the forceful and endless OCD, the soul crushing paralyzation of bipolar disorder, memory deficits of the TBI, and the constantly aching and movement-limiting back problems, full-time employment still consumes most of the day every day. After gaining the undergraduate degree, the graduate degree, and working for over fifteen years, I'm still going strong and am as energetic and passionate about making the world a little better. The seemingly insurmountable problems were all transcended. After the job of running a chemical dependency program for over a decade, I was promoted and became the housing director and oversaw housing at that agency, including the old housing programs I created when I started. Since then, I decided to become a full time psychotherapist and work with people having many issues that are often similar to mine. I continue to engage in a psychotherapy that can be very powerful and very effective at changing lives using empathy and the concept of Antaeus.

It did not all go seamlessly. Does it ever go seamlessly? It took six years to go through undergraduate school. But it was accomplished. It took another six years to get through my master's degree. But both were accomplished. I almost quit many times during each. But they was accomplished – despite all of these issues. Everything started was almost stopped. But they were accomplished.

As it is probably evident from this book, supreme honesty is something that I value very dearly. It is my firm

belief that the truth should be told for truth's sake and if there are repercussions, so be it. At least you are authentic and honest and facing your problems.

Whatever Angelo saw in me in college, I wanted to set the record straight before he took a chance on me in employment. That is why I sat with him in that restaurant before my internship even began and made sure that he knew I had bipolar disorder, OCD, and a severe traumatic brain injury.

His response — a belief in me and a belief that adversity could be transcended — fueled me. And that was it. That helped conjure the last bit of courage that was needed to get knocked down on a daily basis in employment as I had at school and in life in general. In other words, someone believing in you who you find credible — a friend, a Mother, a Dad, a boss, whoever — can ignite that spark and fuel the courage to rebel against misfortune and defy suffering. Eventually you will believe in yourself and you won't need another to believe in you. This is truly a psychological strength that, if developed, will keep you getting up for years to come.

The service performed for others due to the professional confidence he gave was meaningful. And the meaning experienced was transformative: for the people I worked for, work with, and as well as myself.

Service, in whatever form it takes, feels like the highest of callings and has always made meaning for me. That service to others has made all the difference. The meaning derived from it is what empowers to navigate the nightmares on a daily basis. And it is helping others simultaneously. In this way, service is symbiotic and transformative.

Despite all of those maladies, I recreated one social service program —the furniture one. Two others were started and created having solely the manuals from the state.

The state of New York was kind as well. I felt nauseous with nerves when they asked me to present on the ability to get people with severe chemical dependency issues employed and on the success of the original housing programs I spent so much time creating. The big presentation to OASAS was at their state headquarters in Albany. I very, very nervously read a meticulously worked on ten page speech in front of the director of housing and many of the other high-ranking officials there. They were wonderfully complementary. It was a very meaningful moment and one that I feel eternal gratitude for.

This gratitude extends also to the fact that OASAS doubled this program in a mere four years of running it. The agency got five more beds — or apartments — that had a different set of criteria for admission. This was starting another program. It is important to always keep in mind, though, that there was and is not a single day of doing this work that I was not plagued by every one of these problems. It is possible to overcome your problems and achieve your goals.

In 2011, after working in social work for three years, an award was given to me from my agency. I will never forget how it was given.

The director of human resources kept asking me to come to a large staff event. Due to the social anxiety, the entire year was spent — like every year — trying desperately to avoid every social event possible. It was required for all the staff. It was also required for all of the staff at sister agencies. There were over one hundred people there and all were social service workers. We went through the day and had a series of seminars. We were in Syracuse and it was a very typical cold and windy and blustery winter day.

Near the end of the day, all of the agencies came together. Leaving early was commonplace due to the socially anxiety. I can remember the director of human resources stating to me, "Now you have to stay till the end, Kurt." That is when I began to suspect something was up. But I did always try to leave early so the comment made sense.

There was a final ceremony during the day wherein each Executive Director got up and spoke. Each gave a beautiful speech about an employee. And each handed out a "most valuable peer" award to one employee at their agency.

"When he came to our agency as an intern," the Executive Director began. She got full attention from me because by using the pronoun "he" she had eliminated around thirty five of the forty workers at the agency. There were only a handful of men at the agency and of those men, even fewer were interns. I met both criteria.

As she went on, I knew full well who she was talking about. Sports were everything growing up and the amount of nerves felt before each game was legendary. But it is uncertain if there was ever as stunned and as anxious a moment in my life — heart pounding, full of anxiety — as when she called on me to receive that award. There were just so many people and there was just so much terror to speak.

"That is why I'd like to give this award for the most valuable peer of our agency to Kurt Warner," she said with a smile.

I was immensely grateful. The award is cherished to this day. But the focus in that moment was that I didn't want to make any mistakes receiving it as nervous as I was. It was only about a minute-and-a-half between the realization that I was selected as the most valuable peer and the time to walk up to receive the award. Nothing had to be said — to my eternal gratitude. Rather, all that had to be done was to walk up, take the award, shake her hand, and go back to the seat. However, my heart was beating so hard that I think I could hear it. And chemicals and neurological responses were animating my interior.

Fortunately, I did not fall or stumble on legs that felt like jelly. I took the award and shook her hand and thanked her. That award has been displayed with immense pride ever since. I got the award for most valuable peer in my agency despite the OCD, despite the bipolar disorder, despite the traumatic brain injury, and despite the back pain. Each of these giants of suffering was like a plague every step of the way. But, to quote Mother Teresa, despite adversity, I was able to, "do it anyway."

After leaving that job, I became a therapist. I am supervised by an LCSW at an agency in upstate New York and by an LCSW at an agency in New York City. There is deep joy felt in working with people of all kinds to utilize their strengths and help them battle their conflicts to ultimately better their lives. My openness with myself about being thrown to the ground and understanding of how that feels has equipped me with the knowledge and experience needed to empathize and connect with virtually any person with whom I am fortunate enough to work. The patients work very hard to improve their lives and I feel blessed to work alongside them by giving them resources, empathy, and by using a wide variety of therapeutic skills and approaches to empower them in their battle to lessen their suffering that I am all too familiar with in my own way.

In other words, I have been able to, thank God, do it anyway at work. Severe issues were transcended in that I have been able to work around them. Each issue has made me stronger. It is unknown if I will be able to continue to transcend these issues for the rest of my life, of course. But ways were found to circumvent every obstacle so far and I have found a way to live a very profitable life despite them. Since lithium, the bipolar disorder has ceased and that was one of the biggest pieces of the puzzle.

However, the other three giants continue to serves as plagues each and every day. Unless these giants become too severe, work will always be a very high priority. The therapy of work is meaningful and can be as effective a treatment as any, except for lithium, writing, Mom and Tanya. The meaning and purpose that employment has given are tremendous assets in the battles against these maladies. Work gives purpose and makes time go by in a way that enables me not to notice my issues so much. It puts the focus away from the self and onto others.

You can succeed in your life, too. If you run toward your problems and use your ingenuity to overcome the obstacles you face, you can become stronger as well. It is hard to believe at first but it can happen. It's having the courage to face your problems and taking those first steps that often prove to be the biggest deterrent.

I have succeeded in other arenas, too, despite these problems. While social work is my purpose, writing is my passion and amongst my very favorite things to do. Writing is amongst the greatest assets.

In college, a short story was published in the college's literary magazine. This was as exciting as it gets.

In graduate school, a professor and I teamed up with another student. We each wrote a section of an academic article to the prestigious *Disability and Society* journal. To our delight, it got published. It is called, "Mentalism, Disability Rights and Modern Eugenics in a Brave New World." It is in an international journal and being published in what the professor said is a prestigious journal was a new accomplishment in my writing career.

These were incredible accomplishments and gave

confidence. However, it was beyond fulfilling and incredible when I was able to sign a document that stated that my writing will be in a book.

In Fact Books (of the Creative Nonfiction Foundation) published a piece written about OCD in a book about mental illness. It is called "The Dictator in My Head." They published it in a book called *Same Time Next Week: True Stories of Individuals Working through Mental Illness.*

Memory is solidified by emotion. It is no surprise that that the day the notification of publication in that book remains very vivid. This phone call was made with the excitement of a kid on Christmas morning.

"Mom! Mom! I did it!"

"You did what, honey?" Mom asked.

"I'm in a book! I got published in a book! I'm so excited!"

"For what?"

"It's an article in a book about mental health. I can't believe it, Ma! And to top it all off, the publisher is out of Pittsburgh!" As an avid sports fan, much attention is placed on watching almost every Pittsburgh Penguins, Pittsburgh Pirates, and Pittsburgh Steelers game. Pittsburgh sports were always more dear even though I grew up closer to Philadelphia and most of the people were Philadelphia fans. The publisher being out of Pittsburgh made it even better.

"I'm so happy for you, honey!" Mom said sincerely.

I worked closely with an editor. She was great and her acumen was especially enjoyed a great deal. After that, it was published. The day I got to do a book signing at the same Barnes & Noble from which I built my library was a dream come true.

In January of 2021, I was accepted for a new, full-length book to be published. It is called *Utopia Realized: In Search of a Just Society* and is the vision of a modern day utopia.

In February of 2024, I was accepted for another new, full length book to be published. It is called *False Idols: How Diversion is Destroying Democracy* and argues that distraction diverts us from our civic duty to one another.

To date, I have written sixteen manuscripts. Seven are narrative nonfiction or nonfiction. Nine of these books are fiction and two of those were rejected by somewhere around one hundred literary agents or publishers. These rejections have made me edit them more carefully and improve them — have made them stronger. In addition, I have the two aforementioned published articles and the one novel that will be published soon. I write each and every day in my journal and have several shelves worth of journals chronicling every day in my life since 2003, after the brain injury. I was also able to work with and sign with a literary agent.

In short, I consider writing a keystone of my existence. Writing is fulfilling in all ways and any rejections received are taken in stride. I learn from them rather than let them hurl me to the ground. Writing provides meaning and validates my existence whether it is about some fictional and allegorical world I create or some nonfiction issue or cause to which I am devoted. It is purpose and I will write as long as God allows me to do so for the depth, introspection, and critical thought it cultivates along with many other benefits. I use writing therapy with those clients who are amenable to it and find that writing is an extremely effective tool for change.

The focus of this chapter was not meant to be in any way bragging or self-promoting. Rather, it was meant to show that despite the very serious problems you have read about and despite being continuously thrown to the ground, a great deal was able to be accomplished. The hope is that it will inspire you or your loved ones to do the same no matter how impossible their plight may seem. I am not unique in any accomplishment. It is possible for you, too. It takes a different way of looking at it and approaching it. And if you're willing to view your pain as your strength, be willing to get up and get stronger when you are knocked down, and summon all of the resources you have, you may find that you have capacities and abilities you never knew before.

Everyone who has deficits also has assets. Yes, bipolar disorder, OCD, an injured back, and a severe traumatic brain injury are deficits. But I also had Mom, Tanya, Angelo, Lithium, writing, and meaningful work. These are the vast bulk of what give life both meaning and joy and helped to counteract the endless plague of problems.

These assets and a willingness to constantly get back up and learning from it after getting knocked down are how these nightmares were able to be transcended.

The statistical chances that I should be able to do what I am doing are remarkably slim, which will be further discussed in the afterword.

The specific formula presented here obviously may not work for everyone. But the general formula can work for everyone. Everyone has to cultivate and define their own assets. If a personal inventory is taken and your assets are developed and your vulnerabilities confronted, it can enable you to transcend — or at the very least improve — your life no matter what disorder, job loss, relationship struggle, or other problem you may have.

However, you must be willing to get knocked down and learn from getting knocked down to find this hope.

VII

DEATH

THE ONLY THING THAT is certain in this life is death. From the second we are born into this world, the only thing that we can count on is that we will die. Death is the only immutable truth. No one is spared death and it comes for us all. It is the end of every hope, every desire, and every meaningful venture that we have in this life. At the moment of our birth, death sits by us like an hourglass holding the sands of time in its hands.

The fact that we know that every breath we take is finite cannot help but cloud, consciously or unconsciously, everything that we do. Whether it is the families we create, the projects that we embark on, or the hobbies we undertake, they all have one ultimate conclusion. That conclusion is that they will cease to be just as we will cease to be.

Therefore, death intrinsically affects the meaning that we make of our lives. How can it not? Life without death would be like playing a football game without time limits. Can yous imagine plodding around on this earth in these bodies with all of their frailties for all eternity? I don't know about you, but just writing that line provoked anxiety. The concept of going on forever in a world so full of flaws, pains, and disappointments seems utterly overwhelming.

However, death remains an almost universal fear in many cultures, and especially in Western cultures. We have all been at family gatherings, organizational gatherings, and other places where in talking about death was taboo. Many of us grow up being afraid to utter the word. We simply don't confront it.

Death, though, does not care. Death seems to find our cultures and our belief systems and anything else we find dear irrelevant. It is the immutable truth. We are all born to die. This is a nonnegotiable part of the contract of life. So the way we approach it, then, seems to be paramount to how we experience and view our lives.

John Donne, an English poet in the late 1500s and early 1600s, first began to affect the way many of us view death because of the impact of his words in our culture. He wrote,

Each man's death diminishes me
For I am involved in mankind
Therefore, send not to know
For whom the Bell tolls
It tolls for thee.

I remember being very attracted to these lines. Up until reading them death was viewed as an inherently solitary venture. However, Donne is noting the universality of death. In the first part of the poem, he said that none of us are islands in ourselves and that we are all part of each other. This concept radically altered my perception of death. Donne was saying that the death of one of us diminishes the death of all of us and that we are all in this together. So when one of us dies, a part of all of us dies.

Viewing humanity as a team, and death as the opposition who is trying to destroy our team, forces us to re-examine how we view death. Donne's vision was instantly embraced albeit rejected and reconsidered during parts of my life. However, these examinations and re-examinations of death enrich us as human beings and are paramount to our existence.

American poet William Cullen Bryant, who wrote in the 1800s, had another extremely impactful way of viewing death. There was a great deal of consolation to be found in Cullen's views on death. In fact, it was so impactful that I read it to Mom when she was in hospice when we were both fully cognizant that she would die of the cancer that plagued her.

Cullen viewed death as a way of us sleeping forever in

That innumerable caravan, that moves
To that mysterious realm, where each shall take
His chamber in the silent halls of death.

He meditates on death not as an evil or bad or terrifying thing, but as a natural part of life. There is no antagonism or overwhelming anxiety about death because it is an inevitable part of life and we've known about this contract of existence since the start.

Cullen's depiction of death also resonated greatly with me. It was the acceptance. It was the acceptance in the way that Seneca or the Stoics accepted death that seemed to resonate. Old age, infirmities of all kinds, our bodies breaking down are inevitable. Why not accept this inevitability because we are all in it together?

Mom always enjoyed the poem as well. That's why it was read it to her in the hospice. She appreciated it and we talked a great deal about death while she was just days away from dying. I would never trade one moment of those talks or that time with her for anything in the world. My evolving view of death changed in those fourteen days as much as they changed in the previous thirty-five years.

"Well, let's talk about the taboo issue, Ma. Do you fear dying?" I asked her one night in the hospice after she had been there several days. Mom was in the bed and I was ensuring that she got whatever she wanted from the hospice whose employees were kind and exceptionally competent at their jobs. The room smelled of ether and it was connected to many other rooms that had many other people who were suffering from an incurable disease or some malady wherein having a comforted death was the best and often only humane option.

She looked at me very seriously and very weakly. Mom was starving to death because the cancer was blocking her ability to eat and retain nutrients.

"Well, everyone fears dying on some level, honey," she said.

"You don't seem to be afraid though, Mom."

"What use is there in being afraid?" She said matter-of-factly. "And why would I be afraid? I had a good life and did nothing consciously wrong to anyone else and have treated everybody around me well. I did everything possible and have no regrets about that."

I paused a moment and said, "Well, you know, like Shakespeare says, 'for in that sleep of death what dreams may come.' Are you at all worried about that? Are you at all worried about what could come next?"

"No, not really. Nobody has any control over what happens next. And I'm not really sure about any of that stuff, anyway."

"What about your Roman Catholic background, Ma?" She grew up in an Italian family who was Christian and specifically subscribed to the Roman Catholic Church. Mom never missed a Sunday, although she was extremely critical of the way the Church represented Christianity.

"I have no control over any of that. I'm not worried about it because I've done everything I could. Sometimes, I think that we just die and that's the end of it. If we don't, that's okay too but I'm not particularly interested in any of that."

I sat in awe of Mom in her view of death. It changed me because she didn't have any particular reservations because she knew it was inevitable. To illustrate this, Mom got very sick around Christmas time with ovarian cancer. Her stomach filled up with a fluid, called ascites, that ovarian cancer makes and it made it difficult for her to maneuver and do things. She did not know what it was at first and was unwilling to go to the doctors to find out. In order to finally convince her to go, I had to drive down from New York to Pennsylvania and tell her I wouldn't leave and until she went. When she did go, we sat in the hospital together and she received the tests. When the tests came back, the doctor said that she had ovarian cancer. After he explained this to her and left the room, tears flooded my eyes.

Mom remained composed like a Stoic philosopher. I can remember her just looking at me and saying, "Well, Kurt, did you think I was going to live forever?"

This was how she dealt with pain or fear across the board. She confronted death with acceptance. Her view echoed the same beautiful view of death that William Cullen Bryant expressed in Thanstopsis. It echoed the same greatness of Seneca as he accepted his fate after the Emperor Nero ordered him to commit suicide for a crime that he did not commit. It echoed courage and, what Hemingway called, "grace under pressure."

I was with Mom every day for the thirteen days it took for her body to starve to death in that hospice. I held her hand as she died and spent every moment possible with her in the nine months that we she knew she had cancer. The earliest days in the hospice were the easiest for her to engage in conversation and we spoke a lot about her life and she thought about death. She was an extremely authentic person even when it came to death. She faced it and she embraced it and there was no fear that could be perceived by those around her. I was with her in the moments that she left this life and she remained just as strong in those moments as in the moments discussed here. She endured a great deal of pain from the cancer and from the starvation and she faced all of it with only a minimal amount of pain killers.

Her death was profoundly impactful. Mom was my best friend. We were always close, but after suffering a profoundly horrible and detrimental injury in my teens, I had to relearn how to do everything again. This was like becoming a child again and brought us much closer and we remained very close until she died. She was, in many ways, the keystone upon which my life was built and when she died there was a feeling of being lost that pervaded everything. My identity was altered and ways to re-create who I was had to be found. This started with accepting her death and accepting death in general as a natural part of existence.

Reading a great deal about dealing with death consumed my time after Mom died. I comforted myself with books and with the concepts in books and came to Mom's realization that nobody really knows anything about what happens after this life. This was very comforting because some of the cultural and contemporary depictions of what happens were disconcerting to say the least.

As a social worker, this made me realize how incredibly disconcerting it was that we as a society do not communally explore and seek to understand death in the same way that John Donne implored us.

Only a few months after Mom died, Dad called. He was about ten months younger than Mom and I had been going back and forth from New York to Pennsylvania to help him after she died.

"Kurt?" Dad started every conversation saying in a very gruff voice.

"Yes, Dad," I said, "are you calling about the slate of games today?" This was a reference to the NFL games as Dad was a staunch football fan.

"It's Sunday?" Dad said. As he said this, I knew something was very wrong. He never missed a Sunday and he lived to watch those games. He called and we spoke every week about who was the better team and what player was going to outperform the other. It was the main way that we bonded and so it was an extremely important part of our relationship.

"Are you okay, Dad?"

"Of course! I'm fine."

"Well, you don't sound fine. Your voice has a certain little rasp in it today, Pop. You sure nothing is up?"

He paused for a bit and this was very unlike Dad. The expectation was for him to roar back and say something to the nature of, "I sound funny because my team is going to lose" and trying to take the emphasis off of the subject.

"Well actually, I'm a little bit of a jam."

"Well, what is it, Dad?" was asked very seriously now. Dad never said that kind of thing. I was looking at the clock and wondering if there were enough hours to drive back and forth Pennsylvania before the game started that day to help him with whatever he needed.

"Well, I was drinking a little and got a little bit carried away. I was trying to catch Orca because she was running all around the house and hadn't seen her in a while. Anyway, I did see her at one point and made an attempt to get her. But you wouldn't believe how fast that cat is and when I found her she was hiding behind a chair and as I leaned in to grab her she took off and I fell like a ton of bricks to the floor."

"Oh my God, Dad! You break anything?"

"No, no. I'm fine. The problem is I can't get up. I'm on my back and at first I thought it was just because I was a little drunk, but I can't get up at all."

Dad worked on the railroad for about twenty-nine years. In return for his giving all of this time and energy and much of his existence to his job, he was given a body that was almost always in a great deal of pain. He had many back issues, joint issues, and a wealth of other health problems. He was always trying to numb the pain and alcohol was a big part of that attempt. It was very hard for him to get up as he was seventy years old and his body was very injured and pained from all this strife that he experienced.

"Dad, how long have you been lying on your back?"

"I really can't say, son. I believe I've seen two moons go up since I fell, but I really lost track of time."

"Are you kidding me? You been laying there for two days and you haven't called me? Dad, I could've come down and helped you out anytime."

There was a few moments before Dad responded, "Nah, couldn't have you missing work. It was a weekday when I went down and you'd be missing work and time with your wife."

"Missing work? I appreciate that, Dad, but you can't be serious that you were afraid I'd miss some work."

"Yes, you missed a lot of work when your Mom was sick and I didn't want you to miss any more. I also drag you down here almost every weekend to help me get supplies and didn't want to put more on you."

"Listen, Dad, I'm going to call the ambulance right now. I don't even want you laying there another two hours. They'll get you up and if you need medical attention you can get that, too. So, do you even know how long it's been since you've eaten?"

There was silence for a few seconds and then he said, "No idea. I was eating before drinking that day, though."

"Are you hungry?"

"I could eat."

I sent the ambulance to Dad's house immediately and they took him into the hospital. There it was discovered that Dad broke his leg when he fell. The hospital was very afraid that Dad could no longer take care of himself at home so he was sent to a nursing home and rehabilitation center afterward. Dad would never return home from that day forward.

The diagnosis was extremely depressing. First, doctors talked to me about his broken leg and the significant complications he had from the diabetes he had from a lifetime of alcoholism. Then, doctors talked about his heart and the issues that he had with it.

And then, one day, I'll never forget when a nurse came in and said, "Kurt, your Dad has cirrhosis." She was tall and had brown hair and had extremely kind eyes.

"He has cirrhosis?"

"Yes. It is a chronic disease of the liver and it is very serious. It causes a great deal of scarring and damage to the liver and your dad has an advanced stage of it."

I looked around the room and remember thinking that the whole thing seems surreal.

"What does that mean for his health?"

"It means that it is another very significant issue regarding your Dad's care. It complicates some of the other issues and we will do whatever we can to treat it. I just wanted you to be aware of it because it is such a major issue."

I nodded.

Between the cirrhosis, the heart issues, the diabetes, and the wealth of other issues that Dad suffered from, Dad was struggling. On October 26, 2018, I was on my way down to see Dad at the nursing home. I drove down from New York and called the nursing home on my way.

"Hi, this is Kurt Warner. My Dad is staying with you

and I was hoping to see him. I'm on my way down now and will be there in a few minutes. I just wanted to call ahead of time."

"Hi Kurt, we are, umm, tending to your Dad right now," a woman said in an extremely unsure voice. "It would probably be, umm, better if you didn't come just yet."

This seemed very peculiar to me.

"Why? Is everything okay?"

"Oh, yeah, yeah, everything is just fine. We'll see you in a little bit. We are just working to get him eating and ready for the night."

It was about six o'clock at night when the call was placed.

"Okay," I said and began to think of different things I could do for a half-hour or an hour since I was close to the nursing home. Thirty minutes later, another call was received. This was from a male doctor from a nearby hospital.

"Kurt Warner? This is Dr. Turner from Scranton Hospital. Your Dad passed away. He was being transported to the hospital from the nursing home. He is still here and we have not called the coroner yet. Would you like to come and see him one last time or would like us to call the coroner?"

My jaw dropped and tears filled my eyes. "I'll be right there," I said immediately.

I saw Dad's body that day and, as with Mom's body, it is something that I will never forget. There is something surreal and unimaginable about death that you don't really know until you're face-to-face with it. I remember looking at Dad and being overwhelmed with feelings of grief and loss.

Both of the deaths of Mom and Dad left an indelible effect on both my psyche and emotions. Up until my parents left this earth, my conceptions of myself were rooted in them. In other words, Mom and Dad were always a very large part of my identity and when they left this life I was forced to confront that hole in my identity as well as re-conceptualize and confront the concept of death.

I struggled with this for a long time afterward. My behavior changed at home and at work. Nihilism was all consuming. There was no longer interest in many of the things that were interesting before. Worked seemed meaningless to me. My relationship with Tanya remained very strong but I found myself pulling away and wanting to just be alone all the time. And in that solitude, I found myself gravitating toward self-destruction. This was perceived as the unconscious mind leaning toward death — the Thanatos — rather than away from it and I embraced this view.

The adversity of losing loved ones changes you. It brings with it a pain that is visceral and overwhelming and that seems eternal. It clouds your thoughts and blocks your vision by replacing it with a visceral depression that upends all of your hopes and dreams and values. There were a lot of conversations like this with my wife,

"What do you want to do this weekend?" she asked very optimistically.

I turned her and shook my head and replied, "Sleep, if I'm being honest."

"Well, how does sleeping help?"

"It delivers me and gives a sanctuary from the here-and-now."

"Well, that deliverance does not seem to be helping you."

"I'll let you be the judge of that. But as far as I'm concerned, sleep provides a small taste of what Mom and Dad got. It lets me flirt with death for a little while and I prefer that to this," I said and waved my hand in the air around me.

Sleep consumed my time. Whatever responsibilities that existed in the conscious world were hurriedly and haphazardly completed so my reward could be attained. I returned to the safety and the sanctuary that sleep is. It disrupted my professional life and it disrupted the relationship I have with Tanya. But it is what was longed for and what was wanted and this fixation was indulged as much as possible.

Put simply, the pain of not having two people who were closer than most anyone was crushing. Any kind of death is most certainly crushing. It overwhelms your energy and distorts your thought. I began going for long walks and embracing meaningless activities that pass time. And on those walks and during those meaningless activities, my brain constantly thought. It thought about the meaning of death and the absurdity of life and what death means to life. This shifting thought, over several months, created a deep shift in consciousness.

The values that compose my existence, in particular, began to shift. And as those values shifted, I began to see the transformative power of death.

What is meant by saying that my values shifted? I mean that death turned down the volume on the way everything else was perceived. Conceptually, I knew full well that death existed and was often thought about prior to my parents dying. During all of the struggles that are detailed in this book, death was thought about often. However, thinking about it and experiencing it are two very different things. So when death knocked on the door, it sunk many of the preconceived notions in my mind. And after those notions sunk, I was forced to create new notions. I created new notions not because of desire but because death forced me to re-examine life. This is when things really began to change.

The pain was immense. It was suffocating. It was visceral. But what is worst of all, is that there seemed to be no advantage to feeling the pain. Would it reduce in time? Perhaps. But just wallowing in it was getting me nowhere. This is the point at which the concept of an afterlife wherein we imagine our loved ones playing games and eating and talking together in a surreal and heavenly world took over.

"Well, I'm sure they're in Heaven," Tanya would say to me.

"If there is a Heaven, I am sure that they are in it," I replied with certainty. "But it's not the existence of Heaven that haunts me. It's the fact that all of this life seems based on loss. It's the fact that the concept of death shrouds everything we do and yet we never speak about it or confront it."

"What do you mean, 'confront it'?"

"I mean we spend our entire lives doing everything we can to not imagine or think about death. Yet it lurks behind and haunts everything we do and everywhere we go. But still, we just ignore it! So yes, I obviously think about Mom and Dad being in a happy place or at least a place that's out of pain. But I also think about the fact that death dominates everything and yet we never embrace it."

"Embrace it?"

"Yes, embrace it! We treat death like every other pain we're afraid to face. How often do you hear people talking about any pain that they dread? When people have dental pain, for example, how often do you hear them talk about the nightmarish pain of the drill as it comes close to or hits the nerve? You don't! We run from pain! We run from the fear of pain and we hide the very existence of it from our minds as best we can."

Tanya nodded as she mused over this statement.

"We do. But why would we? Who would run toward pain?"

"Anyone who wants to lessen their pain. Not talking about the monster under your bed when you're a kid makes the monster stronger. Our only option to reducing our pain is to throw the covers off the bed and look under it and see face-to-face that there's no monster there. And if it is there, you'll be able to see its eyes and its mouth and its nose and you'll know that it's not what your brain has made it to be, but what it actually is. Don't you agree that there is power in that?"

As much as the immense pain of loss and death was overwhelming, these conceptions began to break through the darkness. The concepts of death being so fearful or as death being the wellspring for weakness began to fade. Finding strength in death no longer became an oxymoron and new notions began flooding into consciousness for how death could improve our existence rather than terrify and leave us wallowing in incapacitation.

It was then that it became clear that facing our fears of death is like facing our fears of any pain that we have. Our task as thinking beings is to reconceive how we perceive the world around us. We have to twist the kaleidoscope of our minds in different ways so that we can see the designs of life in ways that are not so insurmountable or unbearable. This creation of a different perspective became the new strategy in facing the death of Mom and Dad and in a broader sense, it became the new strategy in facing the concept of death in this existence.

I can remember turning to Tanya and discussing the issue to see how she conceived of it.

"Tanya, is there anything that you see as good about death?"

She paused and thought about it for a few seconds.

Then she replied, "No. Why would death be anything good?"

"Well, there are lots of ways. Do you want to live forever and ever in your current body and in this current life?"

"Not particularly."

"Isn't it only death that delivers us from that?"

"I suppose but—."

"You work with the elderly. You see that all of our bodies inevitably decay and break down with every passing second, day, week, and year. Every moment holds with it decay and fragility and the slow annihilation of all of our abilities, both physical and mental. So then, more life, paradoxically, equals less quality of life. Do you agree that death is then deliverance from that infirmity and that cycle of endless decay and pain?"

"This conversation got awfully morbid," she said with a smile. "I mean yes, I see your point, but I still feel very strongly about living, despite whatever it brings."

"Good. I hope you always feel that way. The concept here is not to argue for death, but rather to argue for not hiding death from your mind. If you can see the utility of death, why do you think that others are so afraid to embrace it?"

Tanya replied immediately. "Because who wants to embrace something that feels so awful to embrace? Why would anybody want to embrace the end of everything they are and do?"

I nodded. "You are arguing for the will to life that

I think it is imbued in most people and that most people embrace it. However, that will to life is not a constant or a permanent fixture in anyone's psyche and when the joys of life are burdened by overwhelming and endless suffering, death can be relief."

Tanya nodded. "Yes, it can be. With the elderly, I see it all the time. There is a point at which they stop seeking to be alive because the pain is too great."

"That's what I mean! All of us innately understand this point and yet none of us talk about it. None of us talk about the fear of death and this lack of discussion only increases our fear. When we do talk about it, we tend to only focus on the fruits of an unknown afterlife that we want to paint to be as wonderful as possible. What kind of approach is this? If we had a child and that child was afraid of going to see a certain teacher at a school, would we let that fear lay dormant and grow stronger as he thinks about it and fears it more and more each time?"

"Of course not. We would have conversations with him in the open about the teacher and see if we could show him that the teacher was not as scary as he thinks."

"Exactly! We would make him confront and respond to what he was so terrified. This is how we deal with pain, not by running from it, but by embracing it! So why is it not the same with death?"

Tanya mused for a few moments and said, "It does not make a heck of a lot of sense, does it? I think it's just natural. People just do it naturally because it feels like the right thing to do."

That's when I realized that the immutable will to life makes death the great fear that we have let it become. I began reading about it and discovered that this will to life is largely cultural. I found that our culture and many other Western cultures contain a fear of death. However, other cultures embrace death and change death into something that makes the culture stronger. Especially in cultures like those in Mexico and much of Latin America, death is often treated with veneration and there is a completely different conceptualization around it. This knowledge, along with my own inquiry, began to change me.

This change became strength. I learned that Mom and Dad completed the human cycle of life and that completion cemented their legacy as wonderful human beings who did great things and had meaningful lives.

I learned that death makes the living stronger by recognizing what we value. It creates new values that emphasize what we truly find important rather than what society tells us to find important or social circles want from us. It creates a new system of seeing what was truly desired in this existence and what truly should be valued. This shift of values makes the time human beings have on earth very short and very precious. These revelations made it clear that no time should be spent quibbling or involved in frivolous activities that have no value to us. Only death can give that gift.

I learned to embrace purpose and meaning. The values that shifted in me created meaning and the meaning created purpose. That purpose is the gas that is in the engine of my dreams and it is what propels me each and every day to do everything that I do. It forces me to create a personal legacy that will serve as a monument to who I am and one day, inevitably, who I was. Mom and Dad created this for their lives and their creation and monument to their existence will live on in me all the days of my life. This unequivocally made me stronger.

In fact, I can honestly say that I have come to believe that death gives life meaning. It gives us a timeframe and structure for which to live our lives. That timeframe and that structure serves to propel who we are and what we want and how we live. Being more conscious of it only enables us and empowers us to live our lives in a more meaningful way. In that way, learn that death is a gift.

I am not alone in this view. Socrates, who is the founder of Western philosophy, had a tremendous impact on everyone who followed him. To this day, Socrates is studied in almost every college philosophy program in the world. He lived around 470 BC and his words and his concepts continue to impact us today and his methods of teaching and relaying information impact us as well. Socrates was quoted in Plato's *Apology*, as saying,

Death may be the greatest of all human blessings.

Socrates, over two-thousand-five-hundred years ago, understood that death is a multifaceted concept that can bring much greatness and that it should not be shunned or ignored. He was therefore able to embrace death and view it without fear and it is that model that he gave Western culture. However, Western culture didn't listen.

Sigmund Freud also saw the advantages that death can bring. He discussed the concept of the death drive. It can be used to explain our destructive impulses, thoughts, and behaviors. In his 1922 book *Beyond the Pleasure Principal*, he would go as far as to say,

> *The goal of all life is death.*

It is hard to deny that this aspect of us exists. But it is cultivated by many other cultures and groups and especially by those who have suffered collective trauma and feelings of pain. The fact that we engage in very destructive behavior is self-evident and the reason that we often engage in destructive behavior can be explained by this concept of death drive. In other words, unconsciously there is something in many of us that seems to embrace death. But still, we do not talk about it in any way publicly.

Lastly, as noted, Seneca was one of the Stoics. The Stoic philosophers believed in logical thought and in living in accordance with nature. In his compilation of letters called *Letters from a Stoic: Epistlae Morales AD Lucilium*, he stated,

> *That day, which you fear has been the end of all things, is the birthday of your eternity.*

True to his words, he faced his death with all of the

courage and virtue that any Stoic could hope.

All of these great men and many other men and women alike have learned and embraced to accept death. They have come to see strength in it due to how it affects how they live and understand life. Mom and Dad taught me a tremendous amount throughout my life. I learned the foundation of everything from them and they were the wellspring for my life biologically, spiritually, and intellectually. When they died, I was really shaken. It was very painful and extremely difficult to endure. However, in time the emotions gave way to the greatest asset that human beings have: higher thought. And higher thought taught me that death is, in the end, a blessing in more ways than it is a curse. It is the great deliverance from a life so long lived and from all the sufferings that life so often entails. For many, it can be considered the reward for getting through such a surreal and Kafkaesque existence.

Death unites us more than any other aspect of our existence. We will all die and so we all have death in common. Since the dawn of civilization, we have tended to focus on what divides us and this is evidenced in the story of humanity. Every history book is wrought with an endless amount of examples wherein human beings divide themselves against human beings. We base this division on virtually anything we can find to base our divisions. Whether it is race or gender or socioeconomic background, whether it is height or what piece of land we were born on, or the level of education we achieved, we will find whatever we can to divide ourselves. Even when we can't find something to divide ourselves, we create it, such as when we divide up into gangs or groups based on any erroneous criteria.

Perhaps it is time that we view death as commonality. Perhaps we can start to look at life in a way similar to what Donne proposed so many years ago. If we can see that death of any one of us diminishes all of us, we can unite and see death for what it is. It is the inevitable step in our existence that should not be feared but embraced.

VIII

CONTRATHERAPY

HOW DO YOU CREATE or change your life? How do you overcome the adversity, whatever form it takes, in your own existence? Let's explore the nature of self-improvement and explore the formula for how you, too, may be able triumph over conflict by becoming stronger from it.

Let's start with the concept of change. The ancient Greek pre-Socratic philosopher Heraclitis said,

You cannot step twice into the same river.

This came from Plato's *Cratylus* and contains a very significant truth. You cannot step into the same river twice because the river is constantly changing and because we are constantly changing. Because we are always changing and the world around us is always changing, change is inevitably at the core of our existence.

However, we generally don't like change. As human beings, change oftentimes is one of the hardest aspects of our existence to endure. In a therapeutic environment, it is routine to see people getting treatment based on changes in their existence is almost universal. So how can something so fundamental to our lives also be something to which we are so resistant? One would think after over two thousand years of civilization, we would have come to terms with the concept of constant change on the level which Heraclitus spoke.

It seems intrinsic that we are wildly resistant to change. I would posit that this is because within change lies conflict. Change brings with it conflict more often than not. And conflict is, perhaps, our fundamental fear. The vast majority of us will resist conflict by any means necessary. And it is this resistance of external conflict that inevitably creates internal psychological conflict in the form of anger and resentment and inaction.

Rationally, though, conflict is an utterly unavoidable aspect of our existence. It is, in many ways, the bedrock of our existence because it is almost always through conflict that things improve. It is almost always through conflict that resolutions come. We are born into conflict as we scream at the top of our nascent lungs and arrive into the absurdity of the world with beeping machines and an audience watching us. Death itself is also conflict. We are forced watch the same bodies we inhabited fail, battle against our will to live, betray us, and send us, as Shakespeare said, shuffling off this "mortal coil." In between life and death is an endless set of conflicts revolving around our basic biological needs each day, our relationships, our hopes, our dreams, and everything in between.

Our desire to find belief systems and viewpoints to

solve our conflicts dates at least back to around 490 BC. This was around when the philosopher Zeno of Elea was born. He is the first person known to utilize the dialectic, according to Aristotle.

Dialectic, according to Merriam-Webster,

> *is any systematic reasoning, exposition, or argument that juxtaposes opposed or contradictory ideas and usually seeks to resolve their conflict.*

Any dialectic will usually utilize two opposing sides to create a resolution. Many of Plato's and therefore Socrates' dialogues utilize the dialectic and it is perhaps the fundamental way that we solve conflict. While Aristotle notes that Zeno is the first person to utilize it, I would argue that every other beating heart on this planet utilizes it each and every day since.

Dialectic, then, has a component that is conflict. Two forces always oppose each other in dialectic and therefore it is implicitly conflict oriented. German philosophers and especially Hegel noted that there is always a thesis, antithesis, and synthesis that can merge two opposing forces in order to find resolution. This concept of contradiction and conflict lies at the heart of any change in our existence.

The basic term for conflict in Latin is *contra*. It literally means, "against," or opposite to." It is, like the concept of dialectic, the vehicle through which change is created. Because change is so essential to betterment and because betterment lies at the heart of therapy, therapy should openly embrace this concept of conflict. The story of Antaeus taught me the value of conflict and the prospect of change. All of that change came through conflict and all of the conflict was based on the paradox that weakness can be strength.

Paradox, according to Oxford dictionary, is

> *a seemingly absurd or self-contradictory statement or proposition that when investigated or explained may prove to be well-founded or true.*

Paradox is a contradiction in itself and therefore the very concept of paradox rests on conflict. The message of Antaeus also rests on paradox. How can weakness create strength? This is one of the underlying theses behind contratherapy.

Contratherapy, as I am proposing it, recognizes that conflict is the vehicle of meaningful change. Paradox can be and very often is a superior form of conflict because it can empower those who lack power. Contratherapy provides liberation to conflict and uses a dialectical and often paradoxical approach. It has not been peer reviewed or empirically tested yet. But it has carried me through the depths of despair and has empowered me to help many others. Let's examine the major themes of contratherapy and how these themes and idioms can affect and improve your life.

Conflict as Freedom

We run from conflict. The utter dread and fear of conflict often creates a veritable mental prison that prevents us from being who we are and doing what we want to do. In fact, it is very often the fear of conflict and not the conflict itself that causes this haze and terror that inhibits our actions. As long as the fear of conflict exists, the mental confinement of our self-created prison exists. No conflict that we have in our lives is ever solved by running from it. If conflict is never faced, we are always imprisoned by the mere conception of conflict and not even of the conflict itself. The concept of running away from or evading the conflict in the many forms that we do is almost always a fruitless endeavor. In fact, outrunning something in your mind is the very definition of absurdity. Facing your fears, then, is the only true pathway to freedom. Therefore, facing conflict is essential to create liberation and separation from any oppressive fear or neuroses. Paradoxically, facing conflict can often be the birth of freedom.

In facing that conflict, we quite often feel weak. But as we embrace that weakness, we can find strength. It is the strength that is hidden paradoxically in the weakness that contratherapy seeks to identify and make flourish. It is this strength that liberates, as it does every time that Antaeus was thrown to the ground.

The freedom implicit in conflict is the choice of how we handle it. There is always a choice when it comes to conflict and embracing the freedom of that choice is imperative to overcoming it. That is to say that we must realize that we have choices within any conflict. As we realize we have choices, our freedom can become overwhelming. However, change occurs if we embrace our freedom and use it to empower us to work through it, slowly and thoughtfully. The freedom of choice empowers us, that is, gives us agency to choose how we handle our conflict and therefore take responsibility over our conflicts. Conflict illuminates our freedom, then, and freedom illuminates our power to create the change that we want to see in our lives.

Conflict as Teacher

Learning and knowledge are what brings light into the darkness of the unknown. When one examines the story of humanity, it is the story of slow enlightenment that has enabled us to extinguish at least some aspects of this darkness. Learning can occur in many ways. Some learn through seeing and others learn through hearing. The amount of ways we can take in information is legion and is very dependent on the person. However, it is my thesis that no greater learning takes place than through conflict. It is through experiential conflict that lessons are most well learned.

We can understand as children that we should not touch the stove. Our young minds can intellectually grasp this generally by the arguments of authority figures – by caregivers warning us of the danger. This is not always an effective learning model because our curiosity and eventual denial of authority can override our obedience.

It is only by touching the stove and feeling the searing burn and recoiling in horror that we truly learn not to do it again. It is only by getting hit that we truly learn to dodge the next punch. In other words, these arguments of authority can be effective but ultimately pale in comparison to learning by experience.

Therefore, the experience of conflict is truly the greatest of teachers. It is by resolution after the conflict that learning truly takes place. In therapy, conflict can be seen not as a weakness or as a horror but as the wellspring of learning and knowledge. These lessons learned can ultimately empower us and help us avoid the pitfalls and horrors of our existence.

Conflict as Hope

If we have a problem and nothing ever opposes that problem, we can expect that problem to go on forever. Therefore it is by opposing that problem, or by conflict, that the darkness of any problem has the possibility of being illuminated. Using this definition, conflict, or opposing your problem, is the wellspring of hope. To quote Shakespeare in his great "To be or not to be" soliloquy in *Hamlet*,

> *Or to take arms against a sea of troubles,*
> *and by opposing end them?*

As Shakespeare makes clear, it is only through opposing our nightmares that we can end them. It is only by conflict that we can end our troubles. This is where the dialectic comes into play. It gives us a mode of mediation that can enable us to resolve conflict. But in order to resolve conflict, all conflict must be embraced. Shakespeare's Hamlet depicts a character who was willing to stare his conflict in the face. He was willing to embrace his conflict and it was only by embracing that conflict that he could create a resolution. We must also be willing to embrace conflict. By facing our bullies and standing up to them, we can achieve a synthesis more often than not that can make our lives livable. It is often through paradox that we can achieve this synthesis.

Conflict as Paradox

Paradoxes surround us. Our lives are riddled with contradictions that give us consternation but that we learn are true. "Stop looking for happiness if you want to find it," is an easy example. We are given an almost constant array of conflicting concepts and on them we have to build our existence.

In *The Myth of Sisyphus*, Albert Camus wrote,

> *I see others paradoxically getting killed for the ideas or illusions that give them a reason for living (what is called a reason for living is also an excellent reason for dying).*

For anything that gives us a reason for living — that gives us meaning — to also be the thing that gives us an excellent reason for dying is the height of paradox. Our very existence is paradoxical in that we are asked to create and build a world for ourselves knowing that we will inevitably die and abandon all that we have created. To create and build and devote oneself to anything that will ultimately be destroyed is absurd and contradictory. Yet this is our lives. It is what we are given and it is up to us to embrace that conflict and to create meaning from it.

The conflict of creating this meaning is, therefore, paradoxical. Conflict can be paradox and paradox can be motivation. If it were not for the paradox that weakness could be strength, I would not be writing this. It may sound like something out of George Orwell's *1984*, but it's true. Weakness can be strength. My very existence is evidence of it. If it were not for the concept that infirmity can be used as motivation and power, the underdog would never win. These are paradoxical statements but they can be absolutely essential in the creation of meaning and in overcoming conflict. In short, the embracing of the paradoxical, or the absurd, can be essential to overcoming our struggles. Running from this absurdity can oftentimes only serve to solidify its survival.

Conflict as Opportunity

We have all heard the idiom, "You can't see the forest through the trees." The meaning behind this is essentially that if you are looking too closely at one aspect of something, you can't see the entirety of it. If you cannot see the entirety of it, your perspective is essentially skewed and distorted. All of our perspectives are instinctively distorted because we are only looking out of one window of life and not being able to see the entire picture. Therefore, this metaphor applies to all of us in many ways.

Perhaps there is no better use of metaphor than through the lens of conflict. Conflict tends to give all of us tunnel vision and inhibits our ability to take a step back and conceptualize the whole picture. Just as a race horse has blinders and is unable to see anything but the goal ahead, we tend to be blinded by conflict and are unable to see the bigger picture of a better life.

Contratherapy raises awareness and enables and empowers us to see the greater picture and the greater meaning that conflict can have. Conflict is often opportunity. Think of any marital relationship. Isn't conflict very often the means by which change occurs? Look at human civilization in its entirety. Where would we be without conflict? Every civil rights movement, every economic rights movement, every workers rights movement is rooted in conflict. In other words, most every moral and meaningful advance that we make as human beings is made through the resolution of conflict.

Therefore, contratherapy argues that conflict is opportunity. It enables us to see the forest rather than just the trees. And by seeing the whole forest, we can make what meaning we want or what meaning we can see out of the conflict we have to suffer. And so while conflict starts as horror, it quickly changes into opportunity.

Conflict as Purpose

Imagine existence without purpose. Imagine getting up and living your life with no drive, no hope, and no goal. Isn't it hideous to think about? The concept of not driving toward something seems a bleak proposition, to say the least.

Conflict carries with it the ability to give our lives the

purpose that we need to create meaning. Examine your own existence. Isn't it the conflict of not knowing what to do with our lives after our education that is what forces us to make the next decision and begin creating our own world? Isn't it the conflict in grade school of wanting to belong that forces us to find the friends who will have an impact on who we are? Who can deny that it is the conflict of deciding who we want to be that causes us to blossom into who we become? Conflict surrounds us in every direction. It does not necessarily have to be a battle or a war for it to be the catalyst of change. Anything that forces us to be in between two opposing sides of what we want is a conflict. And anything that forces us to be between two opposing sides can be an opportunity to create purpose.

The American Heritage Dictionary defines purpose as,

> *the object toward which one strives or for which something exists; an aim or goal.*

Purpose, then, creates the meaning for which we live our lives. It is what we strive for and is quite literally the reason that we want to live. Purpose and the meaning it creates is what enables us to transcend pain, suffering, and almost any obstacle imaginable. It is the building block upon which resilience and hope are built. And one of the most essential ingredients for creating meaningful purpose in anyone's lives is conflict.

As noted, contratherapy embraces conflict. It cultivates the meaning and the purpose that have the capacity to improve our lives. It harnesses conflict and conquers it by salvaging the wreckage of whatever troubles we encounter. It pulls out and salvages and repackages all the raw materials that are necessary to create a purposeful and driven existence. In this way, conflict is not something to be avoided. Rather, conflict is to be embraced because of the fruits that can be created by reconceiving of what has been left behind. These assets can be picked up, acknowledged, and forged into the materials needed to not only transcend one's pain but to overcome it.

Contratherapy's Solution

The concepts underlying contratherapy include conflict and paradox. When conflict occurs in the endless amount of shapes and sizes that it inevitably does in our lives, our impulse is always to run from them. It has been this way since our inception as human beings and one can only imagine our ancestors running as fast and as quickly away from the many threats in the forest or in nature in general. But again, running from any problem serves only to preserve that problem. Running at the problem seems both absurd and contradictory. However, this paradox can be liberating. Running at the problem and embracing the conflict in whatever form it may take is often very necessary to defeat it. Because as Albert Camus once wrote

> *For no matter how hard the world pushes against me, within me, there's something stronger — something better — pushing right back.*

There is some strength that we have that the world cannot take unless we submit to it. We can push back and each can do so in our own personal way utilizing our own strengths to make almost any mountain less daunting and more manageable. It was only by our ancestors stopping and viewing the many threats in the forest that they were able to conceive of what they needed to defend themselves against their early predators. It is only by running toward our issues with all of our strengths and assets and embracing our conflicts with open arms that we can learn to overcome the slings and arrows of a life filled with pain and paradox. Because in conflict there is meaning and in meaning there is peace.

Conflict is as old as living beings. We are but one species that were born into conflict and who can feel its icy breath on our necks in all we do and everywhere we go. This conflict permeates every aspect of the stories we tell. It is through stories – the act of creating stories – spoken and written – that we create the meaning that empowers us to battle the conflict that surrounds us on all sides. Literature and narrative generally reflect reality and reality is undeniably centered on conflict. Therefore, life always contains an antagonist. It is by recognizing and facing this antagonist – this conflict – that we can become whole.

Conflict, then, is ultimately that great light on the hill that enables us to define our lives and fulfill our dreams. In *The Grapes of Wrath*, John Steinbeck wrote,

> *For man, unlike any other thing organic or inorganic in the universe, grows beyond his work, walks up the stairs of his concepts, emerges ahead of his accomplishments.*

Steinbeck was writing the passage in regard to worker's rights and the labor movement, an ongoing conflict that remains relevant today. However, his words are relevant in regard to other conflicts. We as human beings grow beyond the conflicts that we incur and emerge ahead of the strife that pulls us down. It is with this sentiment that we have created all that we have created as a species. It is with this growth and with this transcendence that we can make this a greater existence for ourselves and for the planet. But it is only by embracing conflicts and all of the challenges that they require that we can define and achieve our individual and collective purposes.

Let us go then and embrace the will to conflict. If conflict begins this existence and ends it and fills all the gaps in between, we have only one choice.

We must bring the face of that conflict out into the light rather than let it continue to hide and gain strength in the shadows.

We must embrace it and learn from conflict and better ourselves by our problems rather than repress and hide from them.

Conflict is to be transcended rather than escaped. There are many tools to overcome it. If we utilize those ways, we can find a way to live a meaningful life despite the conflict that plagues us.

Only then can we become like Antaeus.

Only then can weakness truly become strength.

AFTERWORD

THE FULL STORY OF Antaeus may further illuminate the concepts used for personal amelioration detailed in this book. In Greek mythology, Antaeus was a giant. He was the son of Gaia, the goddess of the earth, and Poseidon, the god of the sea. Antaeus was obviously a force to be reckoned with. When your mom rules the land and your dad rules the sea, it is safe to say that you are hard to beat.

Antaeus loved to fight and would fight often. He challenged the passers-by to wrestle to the death as they wandered through his land in Libya.

Every time Antaeus got thrown to the ground, it made him stronger. His strength was renewed by the ground because of his mom and her power over the earth. By getting knocked down or thrown to the ground, Antaeus gained strength.

Antaeus acquired strength from defeat. So can we.

The story of Antaeus is one that needs to be resident in the minds of everyone who is thrown to the ground over and over again in life. The pain of life can be edifying. Every ailment can be learned from and many can be managed or overcome. The lessons we can learn from our pain and our suffering can be our Gaia — our strength. That is, the lessons can be our rejuvenating guide that can enable us to overcome our ailments.

We can all be Antaeus. The more we are thrown to the ground of life, whether by cancer or depression, by a broken leg or by broken dreams, the stronger we can become. The lessons we can learn from defeat are almost always overlooked in our culture because it is a culture that only values victory and winning and teaches that pain and suffering are to be avoided at all costs. This does a disservice to the gifts that suffering can give if they are cultivated. Running from our problems will never solve them or make us stronger to take on new problems. If faced and embraced, however, pain and defeat can offer incredible gifts — at an admittedly painful price — to those who fight to overcome them. Among those gifts include the strength to work around pain and suffering. We can all find ways to work around our pain and our suffering to live meaningful and fulfilling lives. We can also learn to become stronger from our suffering. We can all become Antaeus.

It must be clear this book is not by any means an argument that anyone with a problem can eliminate that problem and should be held to that standard. It is arguing that they can learn ways to transcend them. Anyone who uses crutches to walk transcends the limitations of her broken leg. The suggestion is that anyone with a malady can think around his ailment and make life more manageable if not downright manageable through reason, self-knowledge, and ingenuity. The task may sound like a Sisyphean one. You may not make your problems vanish or even reduce them at first. However, you can become much more able in time. You can get closer to living the life you want to live despite whatever ailment or malady befalls you. This book is meant to make you and those around you see that you are not fully imprisoned by your ailments. It aims to enable you to see that you are stronger and more capable than your infirmities will allow you to see. It aims to empower you to enhance your self-worth by understanding that you are actually stronger and more capable due to the very ailment that makes you feel weak and less capable. It will enable you to see that you are Antaeus. You will find ways. You will get stronger. You will attain what is meaningful.

But none of this can be done alone. There is often a great deal of debt owed to physical therapists, doctors, psychiatrists, and so many other professionals for you to overcome most maladies. Family, friends, and loved ones all serve as strengths throughout many of the worst parts of your storms. If you have a faith in something greater than yourself, that, too, can serve as a great strength to empower you to keep getting up.

It was with this sentiment that I want to end this book: *It is possible to live a life around most problems.*

It is about using your mind and changing your perception.

It is also by being humble enough to ask for help.

RESOURCES

WE CAN ALL BENEFIT from resources to help us get up when we're thrown down. Every community, large and small, has resources. Below are just a fraction of those resources that can help you when you are struggling. These resources exist on national, state, county, smaller community, and individual levels.

Crisis Line: 988 Suicide and Crisis Lifeline: Call or text 988 or chat online at *www.988lifeline.org*

BIPOLAR

American Academy of Child and Adolescent Psychiatry: *www.aacap.org*

American Psychiatric Association: *www.psychiatry.org*

American Psychological Association: *www.apa.org*

Depression and Bipolar Support Alliance (DBSA): 1-800-826-3632

FindTreatment.gov: *www.findtreatment.gov*

Mental Health America (MHA): *www.mhanational.org/conditions/bipolar/disorder*

National Alliance on Mental Illness (NAMI) Helpline: Call 1-800-950-NAMI, text HELPLINE to 62640, email *info@nami.org*, or chat online

National Alliance on Mental Illness (NAMI): *www.nami.org*

National Institute of Mental Health Information Resource Center: Call 1-866-615-6464 or email *nimhinfo@nih.gov* or chat online with a representative Monday-Friday 8:30 AM - 5:30 PM at *www.nimh.nih.gov/site-info/contact-nimh*

SAMHSA Find Support for mental health, drugs, or alcohol visit: *www.findsupport.gov*; National Helpline: 1-800-662-HELP for treatment providers; SAMHSA website: *www.samhsa.gov/mental-health/bipolar*

TRAUMATIC BRAIN INJURY

American Psychiatric Association: *www.psychiatry.org*

American Speech Language Hearing Association: *www.asha.org*

Bob Woodruff Foundation: *www.bobwoodrufffoundation.org*

Brain Injury Association of America: *www.biausa.org*

Brainline: *www.brainline.org*

Brain Trauma Foundation: *www.braintrauma.org*

Centers for Disease Control: *www.cdc.gov/traumaticbraininjury*

Centers for Medicare and Medicaid Services: *www.cms.gov*

Center Watch: *www.centerwatch.com/clinical-trials/listings/condition/149/traumatic-brain-injury*

Department of Veteran Affairs: *www.va.gov*

The Concussion Legacy Foundation: *www.concussionfoundation.org*

The Dana Foundation: *www.dana.org*

FindTreatment.gov: *www.findtreatment.gov*

Love Your Brain Foundation: *www.loveyourbrain.com*

National Alliance of Family Caregivers: *www.caregvier.org*

National Disability Rights Network: *www.ndrn.org*

National Institute of Child Health and Human Development: *www.nichd.nih.gov/health/topics/tbi*

National Institute of Mental Health Information Resource Center: Call 1-866-615-6464 or email *nimhinfo@nih.gov* or chat online with a representative online Monday - Friday 8:30 AM - 5:30 PM at *www.nimh.nih.gov/site-info/contact-nimh*

National Institute of Neurological Disorders and Stroke: *www.ninds.nih.gov*

National Rehabilitation Information Center: *www.naric.com*

Social Security Administration Office of Public Inquiries: *www.ssa.gov*

State Chapters of the Brain Injury Association of America: *www.biausa.org/find-bia*

Wounded Warrior Project: *www.woundedwarriorproject.org*

OCD

Anxiety and Depression Association of America: 1-240-485-1001 or online contact form: *www.adaa.org/contact-us*

Crisis Text Line for People with OCD: Text HOME to 741741

International OCD Foundation (IOCDF): 1-617-973-5801, or online contact form: *www.iocdf.org/about/contact/us/*

National Alliance on Mental Illness (NAMI) Helpline: Call 1-800-950-NAMI, text HELPLINE to 62640, email *info@nami.org*, or chat online for support and information about community resources

National Alliance on Mental Illness (NAMI): *www.nami.org*

National Institute of Mental Health (**NIMH**): 1-866-615-6464

SAMHSA Find Support for mental health, drugs, or alcohol visit: *www.findsupport.gov;* SAMHSA's National Helpline: 1-800-662-HELP; SAMHSA website: *www.samhsa.gov*

TLC Foundation for Body Focused Repetitive Behaviors: *www.bfrb.org*

CHRONIC PAIN (BACK PAIN)

American Chronic Pain Association: *www.acpanow.com*

Centers for Disease Control and Prevention: *www.cdc.gov/chronic-disease/living-with/*

National Fibromyalgia and Chronic Pain Association: *www.askjan.org/disabilities/chronicpain.cfm*

US National Library of Medicine, Medline Plus: *www.medlineplus.gov/chronicpain.html*

BEREAVEMENT

AARP: *www.aarp.org/home-family/caregiving/grief-and-loss/*

Grief.com: *www.grief.com*

Grief In Common: *www.griefincommon.com*

Grief Recovery After a Substance Abuse Passing: 1-302-492-7717

GriefShare.org: *www.griefshare.org* or call 1-800-395-5755

Hospice and Community Care: *www.hospiceandcommunity-care.org*

Open to Hope: *www.opentohope.com*

Suicide Loss Survivors: *www.suicidepreventionlifeline.org/help-yourself-loss-survivors*

Web Healing: *www.webhealing.com*

OTHER HELPFUL RESOURCES

Alzheimer's Association: 24/7 Helpline: 1-800-272-3900

Boystown USA: Your Life Your Voice Helpline for children, parents, and families who are struggling with self-harm, mental health disorders, and abuse: 1-80-488-3000 or text VOICE to 20121

Elder Care Locator: 1-800-677-1116

LGBTQ+ Trans Lifeline: 1-800-565-8860

National Child Abuse Hotline: 1-800-422-4453

National Domestic Violence Hotline: 1-800-799-7233 or text: LOVEIS to 22522

National Sexual Assault Hotline: 1-800-656-4673

National Institute on Alcohol Abuse and Alcoholism: *www.niaaa.nih.gov*

Opioid Treatment Program Directory by State: *www.smasha.gov/find-help/national-helpline*

Psychology Today: *www.psychologytoday.com*

Schizophrenia & Psychosis Action Alliance: 1-800-493-2094

The Trevor Project Lifeline: 1-866-488-7386

ACKNOWLEDGMENTS

THANK YOU ANTHONY RAYMOND Michalski and Kallisti Publishing. From our very first correspondence, I was overwhelmed by Anthony's humanism, kindness, and dedication to producing quality literature that makes a difference in people's lives. Kallisti Publishing exemplifies the freedom and power of the independent press to shine a light on important but often unheard voices.

ABOUT THE AUTHOR

KURT WARNER GRADUATED *SUMMA cum laude* with a Bachelor's degree in English literature from King's College in Pennsylvania and graduated with a Master's in social work from Binghamton University. Mr. Warner was published in the academic journal *Disability in Society* as well as in a book entitled *Same Time Next Week: True Stories of Working through Mental Illness*. He is currently working as a psychotherapist helping individuals struggling with mental health issues. He has upcoming books called *Utopia Realized: In Search of a Just Society* and *False Idols: How Diversion is Destroying Democracy*.

outlining the events, trends, and themes which led from academic and social success (in HS), to increased maladaptive behavior, more limited success, and previous risk taking/lapse in judgement leading up to injuries in Spain. Didn't have to be that way.

- Assertiveness
- priorities
- loyalties
- interests
- friends, family
- discipline
- (- sexuality)
- beliefs

Made in the USA
Middletown, DE
25 October 2024

63007322R00144